Handbook of The Cleveland Museum of Art

HANDBOOK

The Cleveland Museum of Art/1966

Contents

Ground Floor

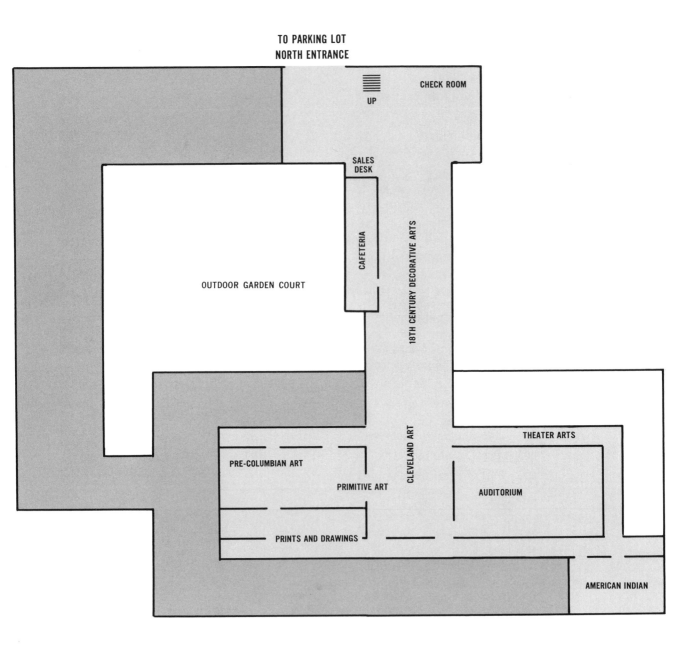

TO PARKING LOT
NORTH ENTRANCE

CHECK ROOM

UP

SALES
DESK

CAFETERIA

18TH CENTURY DECORATIVE ARTS

OUTDOOR GARDEN COURT

CLEVELAND ART

THEATER ARTS

PRE-COLUMBIAN ART

PRIMITIVE ART

AUDITORIUM

PRINTS AND DRAWINGS

AMERICAN INDIAN

Gallery Floor

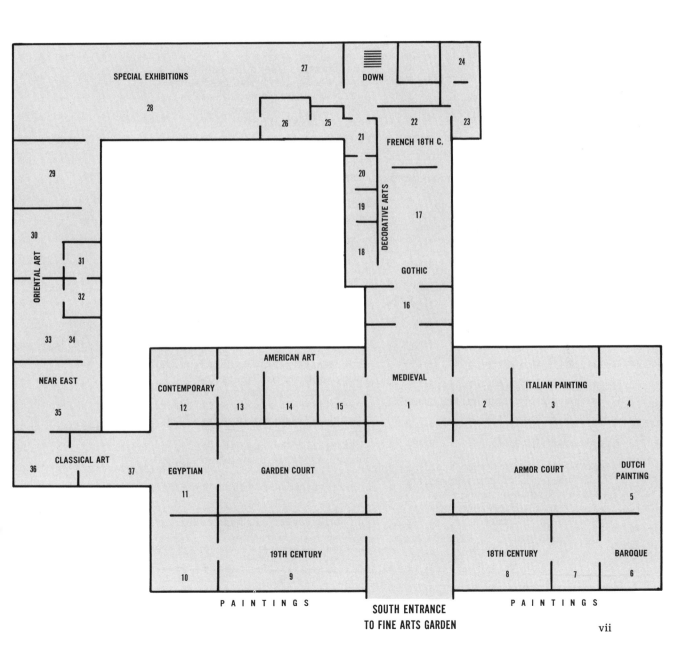

SPECIAL EXHIBITIONS

27

DOWN

24

28

26   25   22   23

FRENCH 18TH C.

21

29

20

DECORATIVE ARTS

19   17

30

ORIENTAL ART

31

18

32

GOTHIC

33   34

16

NEAR EAST

AMERICAN ART

35

MEDIEVAL

ITALIAN PAINTING

CONTEMPORARY

12   13   14   15   1   2   3   4

CLASSICAL ART

DUTCH
PAINTING

36   37   EGYPTIAN   GARDEN COURT   ARMOR COURT

11   5

19TH CENTURY   18TH CENTURY   BAROQUE

10   9   8   7   6

P A I N T I N G S   P A I N T I N G S

SOUTH ENTRANCE
TO FINE ARTS GARDEN

vii

General Information

MUSEUM HOURS

Open free at all times
Closed Monday
Tuesday 10 a.m. to 6 p.m.
Wednesday 10 a.m. to 10 p.m.
Thursday 10 a.m. to 6 p.m.
Friday 10 a.m. to 10 p.m. during lecture
    season; 10 a.m. to 6 p.m. in summer
Saturday 9 a.m. to 5 p.m.
Sunday, New Year's Day, and Memorial
    Day 1 p.m. to 6 p.m.
Closed July 4, Thanksgiving and
    December 25.

RESTAURANT

Tuesday through Friday luncheon is
    served from noon to 2:15 p.m.; on
    Saturday from 11:45 a.m. to 2:15 p.m.
Afternoon tea is served from 3:15 to
    4:45 p.m. Tuesday through Friday; and
    3:00 to 4:30 p.m. on Saturday.

GALLERY ADVICE

Members of the staff are prepared to
assist visitors, but appointments should
be arranged in advance.

SALES DESK

Catalogues, color prints, post cards,
Christmas cards, *Bulletins*, books, and
framed reproductions are for sale at
the desk near the North entrance. A
list will be mailed on request.

LIBRARY

The Library is free to the public at all
times. Books and current magazines
for reference only and photographs for
loan are available. Lantern slides for
loan are on the Library floor. The
Library is open from 10 a.m. to 5:45 p.m.
on Tuesday, Wednesday, Thursday, and
Friday. On Saturday it is open from
9 a.m. to 4:45 p.m. From October
through May the Reading Room is open
Sundays from 3 p.m. to 5:45 p.m. and
Wednesdays from 10 a.m. to 7 p.m.

MEMBERSHIP

Foundation Benefactors contribute
    $500,000
Benefactor Fellows contribute $250,000
Endowment Benefactors contribute
    $100,000
Benefactors contribute $25,000
Endowment Fellows contribute $10,000
Fellows in Perpetuity contribute $5,000
Fellows for Life contribute $1,000
Living or Memorial Endowments
    contribute any sum above $500
Special Life Members contribute $500
Life Members contribute $250
Fellows contribute annually $100
Sustaining Members contribute annually
    $25
Annual Members contribute annually
    $10

Full particulars may be had upon request.

Reading List

GENERAL

Gombrich, E.H.J. *The Story of Art*. London:
  Phaidon Press, 1950.
Janson, H.W. *History of Art*. New York:
  Harry N. Abrams, 1962.
Panofsky, Erwin. *Meaning in the Visual
  Arts*. Garden City, N. Y.: Doubleday,
  1957.
Wölfflin, Heinrich. *Principles of Art
  History*. New York: H. Holt, 1932.

EGYPTIAN ART

Aldred, Cyril. *New Kingdom Art in
  Ancient Egypt*. London: A. Tiranti, 1961.
Edwards, I.E.S., et al. *A General
  Introductory Guide for the Egyptian
  Collections in the British Museum*.
  London: British Museum, 1964.
Gardiner, Sir Alan. *Egypt of the Pharaohs*.
  Oxford: Clarendon Press, 1961.
Montet, Pierre. *Everyday Life in Egypt*.
  London: Edward Arnold, 1958.
Posener, Georges, et al. *Dictionary of
  Egyptian Civilization*. New York:
  Tudor, 1959.
Smith, W.S. *The Art and Architecture of
  Ancient Egypt*. Harmondsworth:
  Penguin, 1958.

ANCIENT NEAR EASTERN
  ART

Frankfort, Henri. *The Art and Architecture
  of the Ancient Orient*. Harmondsworth:
  Penguin, 1958.
Ghirshman, Roman. *Iran*. Harmondsworth:
  Penguin, 1954.
Godard, André. *The Art of Iran*. New
  York: Frederick A. Praeger, 1965.
Parrot, André. *The Arts of Mankind*. Vol.
  I: *Sumer*. Vol. II: *Nineveh and Babylon*.
  London: Thames & Hudson, 1961.

CLASSICAL ART

Bieber, Margarete. *The Sculpture of the
  Hellenistic Age*. New York: Columbia
  University Press, 1961.
Bowra, C.M. *The Greek Experience*.
  Cleveland: World, 1958.
Carpenter, Rhys. *Greek Sculpture*.
  Chicago: University of Chicago Press,
  1960.
Devambez, Pierre. *Greek Sculpture*. New
  York: Tudor, 1961.
Grant, Michael. *The World of Rome*.
  Cleveland: World, 1960.
Hanfmann, George M.A. *Roman Art*.
  Greenwich, Conn.: New York Graphic
  Society, 1964.
Richardson, Emeline H. *The Etruscans,
  Their Art and Civilization*. Chicago:
  University of Chicago Press, 1964.
Richter, G.M.A. *Kouroi*. New York: Oxford
  University Press, 1960.

COPTIC ART

Beckwith, John. *Coptic Sculpture
  300-1300*. London: Alec Tiranti, 1963.
Edwards, I.E.S., et al. *A General
  Introductory Guide for the Egyptian
  Collections in the British Museum*.
  London: British Museum, 1964, pp. 222 ff.

EARLY CHRISTIAN AND
  BYZANTINE ART

Ainalov, D.V. *The Hellenistic Origins of
  Byzantine Art*. New Brunswick, N.J.:
  Rutgers University Press, 1961.
Beckwith, John. *The Art of Constantinople*.
  London: Phaidon Press, 1961.
Meer, Frederick van der, and Christine
  Mohrmann. *Atlas of the Early Christian
  World*. New York: Nelson, 1958.
Rice, David Talbot. *Byzantine Painting*.
  London: Avalon Press, 1948.
Volbach, W.F. *Early Christian Art*. New
  York: Harry N. Abrams, 1961.

THE WESTERN TRADITION

Medieval Art

Beckwith, John. *Early Medieval Art.* New York: Frederick A. Praeger, 1964.

Evans, Joan. *Art in Medieval France.* New York: Oxford University Press, 1948.

Gnudi, Cesare, and Jacques Dupont. *Gothic Painting.* Geneva: Skira, 1954.

Huizinga, J. *The Waning of the Middle Ages.* New York: Doubleday, 1954.

Meiss, Millard. *Painting in Florence and Siena after the Black Death.* Princeton: Princeton University Press, 1951.

Swarzenski, Hans. *Monuments of Romanesque Art.* Chicago: University of Chicago Press, 1954.

Renaissance Art

Berenson, Bernard. *Italian Painters of the Renaissance.* Cleveland: World, 1964.

Burckardt, Jacob. *The Italian Renaissance.* New York: Harper & Row, 1958.

Freedberg, Sydney J. *Painting of the High Renaissance in Rome and Florence.* Cambridge: Harvard University Press, 1961.

Panofsky, Erwin. *Studies in Iconology.* New York: Oxford University Press, 1939.

Pope-Hennessy, John. *Introduction to Italian Sculpture.* London: Phaidon Press, 1955-1962.

Wölfflin, Heinrich. *The Art of the Italian Renaissance.* New York: Schocken Books, 1964.

17th-century to 19th-century Art

Blunt, Anthony. *Art and Architecture in France 1500 to 1700.* London and Baltimore: Penguin, 1953.

Gerson, Horst, and E. H. ter Kerle. *Art and Architecture in Belgium, 1600 to 1800.* Harmondsworth: Penguin, 1960.

Hawley, Henry H. *Neo-classicism: Style and Motif.* Cleveland: The Cleveland Museum of Art, 1964.

Hempel, Eberhard. *Baroque Art and Architecture in Central Europe. . . .* Harmondsworth: Penguin, 1965.

Honey, William Bowyer. *European Ceramic Art from the End of the Middle Ages to about 1815.* London: Faber & Faber, 1949-52.

Jackson, Sir Charles James. *An Illustrated History of English Plate . . . .* London: Country Life, 1911.

Novotny, Fritz. *Painting and Sculpture in Europe, 1780 to 1880.* Harmondsworth: Penguin, 1960.

Rewald, John. *The History of Impressionism.* New York: Museum of Modern Art, 1961.

———. *Post Impressionism from Van Gogh to Gauguin.* New York: Museum of Modern Art, 1956.

Rosenberg, J. and S. Slive. *Dutch Art and Architecture, 1600 to 1800.* Harmondsworth: Penguin, 1966.

Stechow, Wolfgang. *Dutch Landscape Painting of the Seventeenth Century.* London: Phaidon Press, 1966.

Waterhouse, E. K. *Italian Baroque Painting.* London: Phaidon Press, 1962.

Watson, F. J. B. *Wallace Collection— London: Furniture.* London: Wallace Collection, 1956.

Wittkower, Rudolf. *Art and Architecture in Italy, 1600 to 1750.* Harmondsworth: Penguin, 1965.

20th-century Art

Ashton, Dore. *The Unknown Shore.* Boston: Little, Brown, 1962.

Giedion-Welcker, Carola. *Contemporary Sculpture.* New York: Wittenborn, 1955.

Haftmann, Werner. *Painting in the Twentieth Century*. New York: Frederick A. Praeger, 1960.

Henning, Edward B. *Fifty Years of Modern Art: 1916-1966*. Cleveland: The Cleveland Museum of Art, 1966.

Hunter, Sam. *Modern American Painting and Sculpture*. New York: Dell, 1959.
————. *Modern French Painting*. New York: Dell, 1956.

Raynal, Maurice. *Modern Painting*. Lausanne: Skira, 1960.

Painting, General

Clark, Kenneth. *Landscape Painting*. Boston: Beacon Press, 1963.

Levey, Michael. *Concise History of Painting*. New York: Frederick A Praeger, 1962.

Richardson, E. P. *A Short History of Painting in America*. New York: Thomas Y. Cromwell, 1963.

Prints, General

Hind, Arthur M. *A History of Engraving and Etching*. New York: Dover, 1963.
————. *An Introduction to a History of Woodcut*. New York: Dover, 1963.

Peterdi, Gabor. *Printmaking*. New York: Macmillan, 1959.

Prasse, L. E. *The Art of Lithography*. Cleveland: The Cleveland Museum of Art, 1949.

Zigrosser, Carl. *The Book of Fine Prints*. New York: Crown, 1948.

Drawings, General

Sachs, Paul J. *The Pocket Book of Great Drawings*. New York: Washington Square Press, 1951.

Watrous, James. *The Craft of Old-Master Drawings*. Madison: University of Wisconsin Press, 1957.

ISLAMIC ART

Godard, André. *The Art of Iran*. New York: Frederick A. Praeger, 1965.

Rice, David Talbot. *Islamic Art*. London: Thames & Hudson, 1965.

FAR EASTERN ART

General

Lee, Sherman E. *History of Far Eastern Art*. New York: Harry N. Abrams, 1964.

Indian Art

Barrett, Douglas, and Basil Gray. *Painting of India*. Lausanne: Skira, 1963.

Coomaraswamy, A. K. *A History of Indian and Indonesian Art*. New York: E. Weyhe, 1927.

Rowland, Benjamin. *The Art and Architecture of India*. London and Baltimore: Penguin, 1953.

Southeast Asian Art

Frederick, Louis. *The Art of Southeast Asia*. New York: Harry N. Abrams, 1965.

Chinese Art

Cahill, James. *Chinese Painting*. Lausanne: Skira, 1960.

Sickman, Laurence, and Alexander C. Soper. *The Art and Architecture of China*. Harmondsworth: Penguin, 1956.

Sullivan, Michael. *An Introduction to Chinese Art*. London: Faber & Faber, 1961.

Willets, William. *Foundations of Chinese Art*. New York: McGraw-Hill, 1965.

Japanese Art

Akiyama, Terukazu. *Japanese Painting*. Lausanne: Skira, 1961.

Paine, Robert T., and Alexander C. Soper. *The Art and Architecture of Japan*. Harmondsworth: Penguin, 1956.

Warner, Langdon. *The Enduring Art of Japan*. Cambridge: Harvard University Press, 1952.

Yashiro, Yukio (ed.). *Art Treasures of Japan.* Tokyo: Kokusai bunka shinkokai, 1960.

PRE-COLUMBIAN ART

Bennett, Wendell C. *Ancient Arts of the Andes.* New York: Museum of Modern Art, 1954.
Covarrubias, Miguel. *Indian Art of Mexico and Central America* .... New York: Alfred A. Knopf, 1957.
Kelemen, Pal. *Medieval American Art.* New York: Macmillan, 1943.
Kubler, George. *The Art and Architecture of Ancient America* .... Harmondsworth: Penguin, 1962.

ART OF PRIMITIVE PEOPLES

African Art

Fagg, William. *Nigerian Images.* New York: Frederick A. Praeger, 1963.
————, and Margaret Plass. *African Sculpture.* London: Studio Vista, 1964.
Leuzinger, Elsy. *Africa.* New York: McGraw Hill, 1960

Oceanic Art

Guiart, Jean. *The Arts of the South Pacific.* London: Thames & Hudson, 1963.
Linton, Ralph, and Paul S. Wingert. *Arts of the South Seas.* New York: Museum of Modern Art, 1946.

Egyptian Art

2

Ny-kau-Re. Red granite. Egypt, Sakkara, ca. 2500 B.C. 64.90

Panel from False Door of Ny-kau-Re. Limestone. Egypt, Sakkara, ca. 2500 B.C. 64.91

Tomb Relief. Limestone. Egypt, Sakkara, Old Kingdom, ca. 2400 B.C. 801.30

Tomb Stela of Four Persons. Limestone. Egypt, First Intermediate Period, ca. 2200-2050 B.C. 200.14

Amenemhet III. Black granite. Thebes, ca. 1800 B.C. 60.56

Head of Queen Hatshepsut. Green schist. Probably Theban School, early New Kingdom, ca. 1475 B.C. 860.17

Three Gods Bearing Offerings. Limestone temple relief. Egypt, reign of Amenhotep III, ca. 1380 B.C. 61.205

Amenhotep III (wearing the Blue Crown). Granite. Egypt, ca. 1400 B.C. 52.513*

Head of Amenhotep III. Quartzite. Egypt, ca. 1380 B.C. 61.417

Amphora. Pale green-white glass. Egypt, reign of Amenhotep III or slightly later in Dynasty XVIII, ca. 1400-1360 B.C. 140.14

Akh-en-Aten. Sandstone relief. Egypt, Karnak, Amarna Period, ca. 1375 B.C. 59.188

Queen Nefertiti. From the Aten chapel at Karnak. Sandstone relief. Egypt, Amarna Period, ca. 1375 B.C. 59.186*

King's Scribe Amenhotep and His Wife Renut. From family tomb near Assiut. Limestone relief. Egypt, early part of reign of Ramesses II, ca. 1275 B.C. 63.100

Head of a Man. Bronze. Egypt, New Kingdom, Theban School, Dynasty XIX, ca. 1300 B.C. 334.14

The Priest Bek-en-Mut Worshiping a Statue of the Long-dead Tuthmosis III. Painting on gesso over wood. Probably from Thebes, Dynasty XXII, ca. 900 B.C. 353.14

Relief of the Late Period Imitating the Style of the Old Kingdom. Quartzite. Egypt, ca. 650 B.C. 3949.20

Man and Wife. From the Theban Tomb of Mentuemhat. Limestone relief. Egypt, Dynasty XXV, in the style of late Dynasty XVIII, ca. 660 B.C. 49.493

Mongoose. Bronze. Egypt, ca. 600 B.C. or later. 64.358

Boat of Mourners. From the tomb of Mentuemhat. Limestone relief. Close adaptation of a lost original of Dynasty XVIII, ca. 660-650 B.C. 51.282*

Relief from the Tomb of Mentuemhat. Limestone. Egypt, ca. 660 B.C. (details are copies from Dynasty XVIII but the servants are chiefly in contemporary style). 51.284

Female Musicians. Joins to another fragment now in Berlin. Limestone relief. Lower Egyptian School, ca. 350 B.C. 199.14

Horwedja Presenting a Statue to His God. Black schist. Egypt, ca. 500 B.C. 3955.20

The General Amen-pe-Yom. Gray granite. Egypt, Mendes, ca. 275 B.C. 48.141

Notes

Notes

Ancient Near Eastern Art

Gudea, Patési of Lagash. From Tello. Dolerite. Mesopotamia (Iraq), Neo-Sumerian Period, 22nd century B.C. 63.154*

Winged Genie. Relief from the palace of Ashur-Nasirapal II at Nimrud. Gypseous alabaster. Mesopotamia (Iraq), Assyrian Period, 9th century B.C. 43.246

Crouching Woman. Ivory figurine. Syria, Arslan Tash, Phoenician, 9th-8th century B.C. 64.426

Plate. Silver, repoussé and engraved. Phoenician, 7th century B.C. 47.491*

Silver Cup with Hunting Scene. Repoussé and engraved. Northwestern Iran (Amlash?), end of 2nd millenium B.C. 65.25

Gold Beaker. Repoussé and engraved. Northwestern Iran (said to have been found at Marlik), end of 2nd millenium B.C. 65.26

Cheek Plaque of Horse Bit. Bronze, cast and engraved. Iran, Luristan, ca. 1200-1000 B.C. 61.33

Votive Pin (detail). Silver, repoussé and engraved. Iran, Luristan, ca. 1000 B.C. 63.257

Finial in Form of Ibex Protome. Cast bronze. Iran, Luristan, late 7th century B.C. 65.554

Beaker. Silver, repoussé and engraved. Iran, Luristan, 8th-7th century B.C. 63.95

Bull's Head (probably an ornament from a bronze cauldron). Cast bronze. Iran, Urartean, 8th-7th century B.C. 42.204

Ibex Head Finial. Cast bronze. Iran, Achaemenid Period, 6th-5th century B.C. 61.199*

Median Lion Strangler. Lapis lazuli. Iran, Achaemenid Period, 1st half 5th century B.C. 60.175*

Rhyton in Form of Ram's Head. Silver, repoussé and engraved. Iran, Kaplantu, Median, 7th century B.C. 63.479

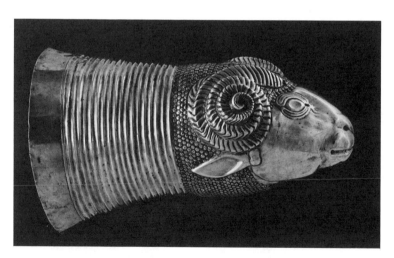

Incense Burner. Cast bronze. Iran, Parthian Period, 1st century A.D. 61.32

Lion Head Finial. Marble. Iran, Achaemenid Period, ca. 5th century B.C. 62.26

Relief Plaque with Royal Hunting Scene: Ardashir II (?) Hunting Lions. Alabaster. Iran, Sasanian Period, late 4th century A.D. 63.258*

Ibex Relief. Carved Stucco. Iran, Sasanian Period, 6th century. 41.24

Rhyton: The Angel Dravspa. Silver, repoussé and engraved, partially gilded. Iran(?), Sasanian Period, 4th-5th century. 64.96*

Plate: The Goddess Anahita. Silver, applied cast relief, chased, engraved, and partially gilt. Iran, Sasanian Period, early 4th century. 62.295*

Plate with Royal Hunting Scene: King Hormizd Hunting Lions. Silver, applied cast relief, chased, engraved, and partially gilt. Iran, Sasanian Period, reign of Hormizd II (A.D. 302-309). 62.150

Rhyton in Form of a Horse. Silver, repoussé, engraved with gold overlay. Iran, Sasanian Period, 4th century. 64.41*

Wine Vessel: Figures of the Goddess Anahita. Silver, cast, engraved, and partially gilt. Iran, Sasanian Period, early 4th century. 62.294

Ewer: Gladiatorial Combats. Silver, repoussé, engraved, and partially gilt. Iran, Sasanian Period, late 4th-early 5th century. 61.200

Textile (detail). Compound twill, silk. Iran, Sasanian Period, 6th-7th century. 51.88

Oval Fluted Bowl. Silver, cast, engraved, and partially gilt. Iran, Sasanian Period, 5th century. 63.478

Textile. Tapestry weave, wool and linen. Iran, Sasanian Period, 6th-7th century. 50.509

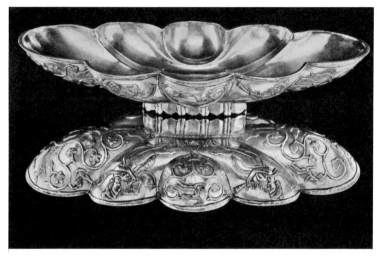

Notes

Notes

Notes

Classical Art

Kouros. Island marble. Greece, ca. 560-540 B.C. 53.125*

Lekythos by Douris. Pottery. Greece, 500-490 B.C. 66.114

Head of Artemis. Terra cotta. Greece, late 6th century B.C. 29.976

Red-figured Krater by the Cleveland Painter. Pottery. Greece, Attic, early 5th century B.C. 30.104

Head of a Goat. Limestone. Greece, Attic, ca. 500 B.C. 26.538

Red-figured Lekythos: Warrior Cutting off a Lock of Hair. Pottery. Greece, Attic, early 5th century B.C. 28.660

Athlete: Mirror Handle. Bronze statuette. Etruscan(?), ca. 300 B.C. (?). 28.659

Athlete: Bronze statuette. Greece, Attic, School of Polykleitos, ca. 450-430 B.C. 55.684*

Head of a Lion. Terra cotta. Greek, from Italy, 5th century B.C. 27.27

Mirror (detail). Bronze. Greece, ca. 470-460 B.C. 50.7*

Charging Bull. Bronze. Greece, Lucania, late 5th century B. C. 30.336

Cista Handle: The Genii Sleep and Death Carrying off Fallen Memmon. Bronze. Etruscan, early 4th century B.C. 45.13*

Grave Monument. Marble. Greece, Attic, ca. 400-350 B.C. 24.1018

Torso of a Standing Nude Man. Marble. Greece, 4th century B.C. 65.23

Incense Burner Supported by Nude Youth. Bronze. Etruscan, 2nd century B.C. 52.96

Standing Lady. Mainland (Peloponnesus) marble. Greece (said to be Alexandria), ca. 300 B.C. or slightly later. 65.24*

Perfume Container in Form of an Askos (Skin). Agate, with gold mounts. East Greek, Amisos (Turkey), ca. 2nd century B.C. or later(?). 64.92

Head of a Barbarian. Marble. Greece, School of Pergamon, late 3rd century B.C. 29.440

Head of a Mule. Bronze. Hellenistic, from Kertch, Russia, ca. 1st century B.C.-1st century A.D. 43.68

Negro Beggar. Bronze statuette, with silver and copper inlays. Egypt, Alexandria, 2nd to 1st century B.C. 63.507

Necklace. From the temple treasure of the lion-god Mahes at Leontopolis in the Delta. Gold, with insets of beryl and amethyst. Egypt, ca. 1st-2nd century A.D. 47.506

Head of a Youth. Marble. Egypt, Alexandria (area of), 1st century B.C. 47.188

Head of a Man. Marble. Egypt, early 1st century A.D. 66.20

Portrait of a Man. Bronze. Roman. late 1st century B.C. 46.28

25

Apollo and Nike. Marble relief. Roman, Neo-Attic School, late 1st century B.C.-early 1st century A.D. 30.522

Torso of Apollo. Marble. Roman, early 2nd century A.D.(?). 24.1017

Portrait Head of a Man. Marble. Roman, ca. A.D. 100. 25.944

Athlete. Marble. Roman, 1st century A.D. 486.24

The Co-Emperor Lucius Verus. Crystalline island marble. East Roman, from Alexandria, ca. A.D. 170-180. 52.260*

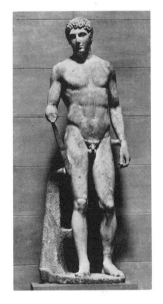

Head of Emperor. Marble. Roman, ca. A.D. 250. 25.945

Tomb Relief. Crystalline limestone. Syria, from Palmyra, ca. A.D. 230. 64.359*

Notes

Notes

Coptic Art

30

Textile. Tapestry weave, wool and linen. Egypt, Greco-Roman style, 3rd-5th century A.D. 53.18*

Dancing Pan. Limestone. Egypt, Coptic Period, 4th-5th century. 55.68

Wood Panel. Egypt, Coptic Period, 4th-5th century. 54.799

Niche. Limestone. Egypt, Coptic Period, 5th century. 55.63

Textile. Tapestry weave, wool and linen. Egypt, Greco-Roman style, 4th-5th century. 1667.16

Textile. Tapestry weave, wool. Egypt, Greco-Roman style, 4th-5th century. 41.293

Textile (detail). Tapestry weave, wool and linen. Egypt, Antinoe, 5th-6th century. 60.273

Textile. Tapestry weave, wool. Egypt, Antinoe, 6th century. 48.27

Textile (detail). Tapestry weave, wool. Egypt, Antinoe, 6th century. 61.201

Textile (detail). Tapestry weave, wool and linen. Egypt, Antinoe.
6th century. 60.275

Textile (detail). Resist dyed on linen.
Egypt, Coptic Period, 6th century.
51.400

Embroidery. Silk on linen. Egypt,
Coptic Period, 6th-7th century. 48.115

Textile. Compound twill, silk. Egypt,
Coptic Period, Akhmim, 6th-8th century.
47.192

Notes

Notes

Early Christian and Byzantine Art

36

Spoon. Silver, gilt and niello. Early Christian, 4th century. 64.39

Bowl. Silver and niello. Byzantium, 4th century. 56.30

Bowl. Silver. Byzantium, 4th century. 54.259

The Good Shepherd and Jonah under the Gourd Vine: Two of a Group of Sculptures. Marble. Early Christian, East Mediterranean, early 4th century. 65.241, 65.238*

Lampstand. Silver. Byzantium, 4th century. 54.597

Pyxis. Ivory. Byzantium, 6th century. 51.114*

Vase. Silver. Byzantium, 4th-6th century. 57.497*

Altar Frontal. From S. Carlino, Ravenna. Marble. Byzantium, Ravenna, early 6th century. 48.25

Chalice. From the Church of
St. Sergius, Rosafa. Silver.
Byzantium, 5th-6th century. 50.378

Pendant with Portrait Intaglio.
Garnet, gold filigree. Byzantium,
6th century. 47.33

Paten. From the Church of
St. Sergius, Rosafa. Silver.
Byzantium, 5th-6th century. 50.381

*Chain with Pendant and Two
Crosses*. Gold with enamel and glass.
Byzantium, probably Syria, early
6th century. 47.35

Necklace with Pendants. Gold, two
garnets. Byzantium, 6th century. 54.3

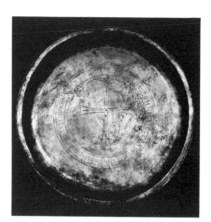

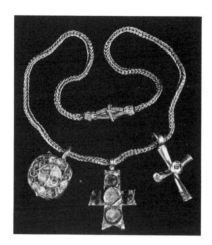

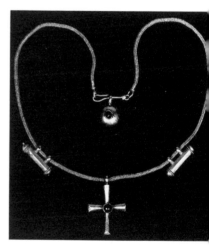

Necklace with Pendants. Gold with garnet. Byzantium, 6th century. 46.260

Rouge Pot. Glass, sapphire, gold filigree. Byzantium, 6th century. 46.427

Monogram of Christ (Chrismon). Gold with garnets, Byzantium, Syria, 6th-7th century. 65.551

Medallion: Bust of Christ. Steatite. Byzantium, late 9th century. 47.37

St. George of Cappadocia.
Quartz (variety of bloodstone).
Byzantium, 10th century. 59.41

Page from a Gospel Book:
St. Matthew. Tempera and gold leaf on
vellum. Byzantium, Constantinople,
1057-1063. 42.1512

Pendant: From the Treasury at Aachen.
1) Relief: Madonna and Child, called
"Madonna of St. Luke." Steatite. Byzantium,
10th century. 2) *Frame with Winged Bull of*
St. Luke on the Back. Gilt silver and pearls.
Germany, Aachen, mid-14th century. 51.445

Single Leaf from the Epistles in a
Manuscript (Pantokrator Ms. 49):
St. Peter. Tempera and gold leaf on
vellum. Byzantium, Constantinople,
11th century. 50.154

Gospels with Commentaries.
Vellum; Greek written in brown
and gold, illuminated with tempera
and gold leaf. Byzantium, 11th century.
42.152

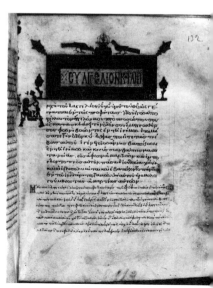

41

Casket with Adam and Eve. Ivory. Byzantium, 11th-12th century. 24.747

Plaque: Virgin and Child Enthroned with Angels. Ivory. Byzantium, 11th century. 25.1293*

Scenes from a Passion Cycle of Christ. Steatite relief. Byzantium, 11th-12th century. 62.27

Notes

The Western Tradition

Medallion with Bust of Christ.
From the Guelph Treasure.
Cloisonné enamel on copper.
Frankish, 8th century. 30.504*

Group of Ornaments.
Bronze and enamel. Gallo-Roman,
2nd-3rd century. 30.230-.234

Crossbow Fibula. Bronze. Gallo-Roman,
late 4th-5th century. 30.227

Well Curb. Stone. Italy, Venice,
8th-9th century. 1678.16

Double Leaf from a Roman Gradual.
Gold and silver on purple vellum.
Carolingian, 9th century. 33.446

Reliquary in the Form of a Book.
From the Guelph Treasure. Ivory
framed in silver gilt. Ivory: Valley
of the Meuse, Liège, ca. 1000.
Frame: Germany, Brunswick,
2nd half 14th century. 2225.30*

*Leaf From a Gradual and
Sacramentary (Trier Codex 151).*
Tempera and gold leaf on vellum.
Austria, Salzburg, early 11th century.
33.447

*Title Page of Abbot Berno's
"Tonarius," Dedicated to
Archbishop Pilgrim of Cologne.*
Tempera and gold leaf on vellum.
Germany, School of Reichenau,
ca. 1020-1030. 52.88

*Gertrudis Portable Altar; First and Second
Gertrudis Crosses.* From the Guelph Treasure.
Gold, cloisonné enamel, semi-precious stones
and porphyry. Germany, Brunswick, Lower Saxony,
ca. 1040. 345.31*, 31.55, 344.31

Casket. Boxwood. England, Anglo-Saxon, ca. 1000.
53.362

Capitals. Stone. France, Collegiale of St. Melaine at Preuilly-sur-Claise, mid-12th century. 30.17

Capital: Daniel in the Lion's Den. Limestone. France, Saint-Aignan-sur-Cher, mid-12th century. 62.247

Châsse. Champlevé enamel on copper over wood core. France, Limoges, late 12th or early 13th century. 54.599

Front of a Châsse: Death of Thomas à Becket. Champlevé enamel on copper. France, Limoges, end of 1st quarter 13th century. 51.449

Cross. Champlevé enamel on copper. France, Limoges, end of 12th century. 24.1015*

Single Page fom a Book on Canon Law (Gratian). Tempera on vellum. North France, ca. 1150-1200. 54.598

The Horn of St. Blasius. From the Guelph Treasure. Ivory. Sicily, 12th century. 2224.30

Capitals. Stone. France, Collegiale of St. Melaine at Preuilly-sur-Claise, mid-12th century. 30.18

Capital. Stone. France, Languedoc, 12th century. 1675.16

Capital: Weighing of Souls. Limestone. France, Loire Valley, early 12th century. 61.407

Engaged Capital: Caryatidal Figure Flanked by Lions. Limestone. France, Burgundian, mid-12th century. 63.477

Priest and Assistants Celebrating Mass: Initial C. Tempera and gold leaf on vellum. South Italy, Benedictine School, ca. 1200. 24.1010

Plaques from a Portable Altar. Ivory. Germany, Rhine Valley, 2nd half 11th century. 22.307-.309

Capital. Stone. South Italy, Atelier of the Cathedral of Monopoli, early 12th century. 55.556

Tree of Jesse: Initial A. Tempera and gold leaf on vellum. Germany, Valley of the Rhine. 1st half 12th century. 49.202

Reliquary. Champlevé enamel on copper over wood core. Denmark or North Germany, 12th century. 49.16

1) *Paten of St. Bernward.* From the Guelph Treasure. Silver gilt and niello. 12th century.
Master of the Oswald Reliquary, German, Hildesheim.
2) *Monstrance.* Silver gilt and rock crystal. Germany, Lower Saxony, end of 14th century. 30.505*

Reliquary. Champlevé enamel on copper. Circle of Godefroid de Claire, Valley of the Meuse, ca. 1150. 26.428

Figure of a Prophet. Champlevé enamel and niello on copper, copper gilt. Germany, Lower Saxony, 2nd half 12th century. 50.577

Portable Altar. Champlevé and cloisonné enamel on copper, over wood core. Germany, Hildesheim, 2nd half 12th century. 49.431

Arm Reliquary. From the Guelph Treasure. Silver gilt and champlevé enamel. Ca. 1175. Follower of Eilbertus, German, Hildesheim. 2223.30*

Single Leaf from a Gospel Book (now Trier Ms. 142): Nativity (recto). Tempera and gold leaf on vellum. Coworker of Hermann von Helmarshausen, German, Saxony, 1170-1190. 33.445*

Apostle from the Cloister of Notre Dame-en-Vaux. Limestone. France, Châlons-sur-Marne, ca. 1180. 19.38

Title Page of "Moralia of Gregorius"
(now Engelberg Codex 20). Tempera
on vellum. Attributed to Abbot
Frowin, Swiss, 1143-1178. 55.74

Mourning St. John from a
Crucifixion Group. Painted wood.
Austria, Southern Salzburg, Lungau,
ca. 1200. 58.189

Mourning Virgin from a
Crucifixion Group. Painted wood.
Austria, Southern Salzburg, Lungau,
ca. 1200. 57.500

Mourning Virgin. Painted wood.
Spain, Castile, ca. 1275. 30.622

Madonna and Child and Saints.
Triptych, tempera on poplar panels.
Berlinghiero the Elder, Italian, Lucca,
active ca. 1200-1240. 66.237

Mourning St. John. Painted wood.
Spain, Castile, ca. 1275. 30.621

Christian and St. John the Evangelist. Painted wood. Germany, Swabia near Bodensee (Lake Constance), early 14th century. 28.753*

Lenten Cloth (detail). Linen embroidery (white on white). Germany, Altenberg a. d. Lahn, 2nd half 13th century. 48.352*

Cross with Mourning Virgin and St. John. Copper gilt and champlevé enamel. Germany, Lake Constance, ca. 1330. 42.1091-42.1093

Angel of the Annunciation. Marble with paint and gold leaf. France, Champagne(?), mid-14th century. 54.387*

Reliquary. Chased copper gilt with cabochons and glass inlay. Germany, Lake Constance, ca. 1330. 32.422

Head of an Apostle. Limestone. France, Toulouse, ca. 1321-1348. 60.170

Central Plaque from a Triptych:
Virgin and Child with Two Angels.
Ivory. France, Paris, Atelier of
Tabernacles of Virgin,
beginning of 14th century. 23.719

Enthroned Virgin and Child.
Ivory. Valley of the Meuse,
mid-13th century. 28.760

Page from Wettinger Gradual:
St. Augustine Introit for the
Mass of Doctors. Tempera and gold
leaf on vellum. Ca. 1330. Second
Master of Wettinger Gradual, German,
Lower Rhine. 49.203

Plaque. Gold with cloisonné and
translucent enamel. France,
13th century. 32.357

Illustration from a Psalter:
Annunciation. Tempera and gold leaf
on vellum. Flanders, possibly Liège,
ca. 1260. 53.148

Madonna and Child with St. Francis, St. John the Baptist, St. James the Great, and Mary Magdalen. Polyptych, tempera on poplar. Ugolino di Nerio da Siena, Italian, Siena, active ca. 1305/10-1339/49. 61.40*

Madonna and Child. Tempera on poplar. Lippo Memmi, Italian, Siena, active 1317-1356. 52.110

Two Female Saints. Tempera and gold leaf on vellum. Niccolo di ser Sozzo Tegliaci, Italian, Siena, active 1334/36-1363. 24.430

Madonna and Child with SS. Catherine and John the Baptist. Marble. Giovanni di Agostino, Italian, Siena, ca. 1310-1370. 42.1162*

Cofanetto. Painted and gilded wood. Italy, Siena, 14th century. 54.600

Angels. Marble. Ca. 1350. Attributed to Giovanni and Pacio da Firenze, Italian. 1621.25, 1622.25

Single Leaf from an Antiphonary: Initial L with Lucy. Tempera and gold leaf on vellum. Master of the Dominican Effigies, Italian, Florence, ca. 1335-ca. 1345. 52.281

Ascension: Initial A. Signed and dated 1308. Tempera and gold leaf on vellum. Neri da Rimini, Italian. 53.365

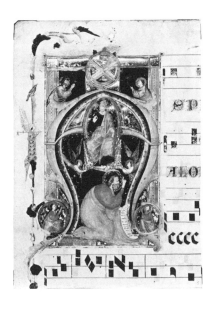

Frontispiece Miniature of the Mariegola of the Scuola di San Giovanni Evangelista. Tempera and gold leaf on vellum. Italy, Venice, first third of 14th century. 59.128

Textile (detail). Diasper weave, silk and gold. Italy (Lucca?), ca. 1300. 26.507

Albarello. Majolica. Spain, Paterna, 14th century. 45.28

Single Leaf from an Antiphonary with Miniature of the Coronation of the Virgin. Tempera and gold leaf on vellum. Late 14th century. Attributed to Master of the Beffi Triptych (Abruzzi), Italian, Tuscany. 53.24

Madonna of Humility with the Temptation of Eve. Tempera on poplar. Carlo da Camerino, Italian, Marchigian School, active ca. 1380-1420. 16.795

The *Resurrection*. Embroidery, silk on linen. Italy, Florence (Geri Lapi?), 14th century. 29.904

Navicella. Pen and brown ink. Parri Spinelli, Italian, ca. 1397-1453. 61.38

Miniature from an Antiphonary: Historiated Initial G with Christ and Virgin in Glory. Tempera and gold leaf on vellum. Ca. 1390-1400. Silvestro dei Gherarducci, Italian, Florence. 30.105

Hours of Charles the Noble: Page 165, The Presentation, by Zebo da Firenze. Vellum, illuminated with tempera and burnished gold leaf. France, Paris, ca. 1400-1408. 64.40

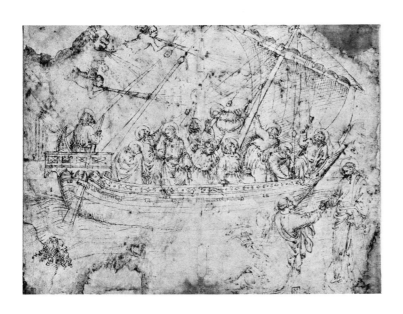

Single Miniature from a Missal:
The Crucifixion. Signed: Nicolaus F.
Tempera and gold leaf on vellum.
Niccoló da Bologna, Italian, Bologna,
active ca. 1369-1402. 24.1013*

Double-faced Portable Crucifix.
Tempera on wood. Italy, Venetian
School, ca. 1370-1380. 43.280

Crucifixion with the Two Thieves.
Pen and brown ink and black chalk.
Altichiero Altichieri, Italian,
ca. 1330-1395. 56.43*

Girdle. Gold-gilt silver,
translucent enamel on silver.
Italy, Siena, late 14th century. 51.30

St. Francis before the Cross. Tempera
on poplar. 1437-1444. Sassetta (Stefano
di Giovanni), Italian, Siena. 62.36

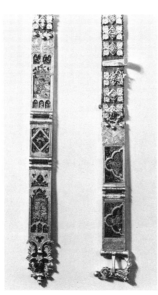

Adoration of the Magi. Tempera on poplar. Giovanni di Paolo, Italian, Siena, ca. 1399-1482. 42.536

St. Catherine of Siena Invested with the Dominican Habit by SS. Dominic, Augustine, and Francis. From the Pizzicaioli Altarpiece. Tempera on poplar panel. Ca. 1447-1449. Giovanni di Paolo, Italian, Siena. 66.2

St. Catherine of Siena and the Beggar. From the Pizzicaioli Altarpiece. Tempera on poplar panel. Ca. 1447-1449. Giovanni di Paolo, Italian, Siena. 66.3*

60

Single Leaf from a Treatise on the Vices with Miniature of Accidia and Her Court. Brown ink, tempera, and gold leaf on vellum. Italy, Genoa or Naples(?), late 14th century. 53.152

Single Miniature under Initial M: The Annunciation. Tempera and gold leaf on vellum. Ca. 1430-1440. Luchino Belbello da Pavia, North Italian. 24.431*

Fragment of a Chasuble with Orphrey (detail). Textile: Diasper weave, silk and gold; Italy (Lucca?), 14th century. Orphrey: Compound twill, silk, linen and gold; Germany, Cologne, 14th century. 28.653

Madonna and Child. Pen and brown ink on rose-tinted paper. Italy, Verona, 1440-1450. 56.42

Textile (Half of a Chasuble). Velvet weave, silk. Italy, Venice, 15th century. 43.66

Single Leaf from an Antiphonary with Historiated Initial with the Virgin as Queen of Heaven. Tempera and gold leaf on vellum. Italy, Lombardy, probably Milan, 2nd quarter 15th century. 28.652

The Coronation of the Virgin. Embroidery, silk, gold and silver on linen. Italy, Florence, style of the school of Lorenzo Monaco, early 15th century. 53.129*

Textile. Velvet weave, silk. Italy, (Venice?), 15th century. 18.310

Two Kneeling Carthusian Monks. Marble. France, Paris, end of 14th century. 66.112, 66.113

Madonna and Child Enthroned. Tempera on poplar. Master of 1419, Italian, Florence. 54.834

62

Single Miniature of a Prophet from a Choral Book.
Tempera and gold leaf on vellum. Ca. 1409-1413. Lorenzo Monaco or Matteo Torelli, Italian, Florence. 49.536

Kneeling Prophet. Gilt bronze. Franco-Netherlands, ca. 1400. 64.360

The Calvary with a Carthusian Monk.
Tempera on oak panel. 1390-1395. Jean de Beaumetz, French. 64.454*

Orphrey: Tree of Jesse (detail). Embroidery (*opus Anglicanum* technique), silk, gold, and silver threads on linen. England, 3rd quarter 14th century. 49.503

Hours of Charles the Noble: Page 395, Descent from the Cross.
By the Egerton Master, with inhabited acanthus border by Zebo da Firenze. Vellum, illuminated with tempera and burnished gold leaf. France, Paris, 1400-1408. 64.40

Figured Medallion. From a group of appliqués. Gold, enamel, pearls. France, Paris(?), ca. 1400. 47.507

Missal, for Paris use (The Gotha Missal): fols. 63v-64r, The Crucifixion and Christ in Majesty. Vellum. Latin written in two columns in red, blue, and brown, illuminated with tempera and gold leaf. Ca. 1375. Jean Bondol and his atelier, French, Paris. 62.287*

Annunciation. Tempera on walnut(?). France, ca. 1390. 54.393*

A Saint Bishop with Donor. Tempera on wood. Spain(?) or Languedoc(?), ca. 1425. 27.197

Table Fountain. Silver-gilt and translucent enamel. France, late 14th century. 24.859*

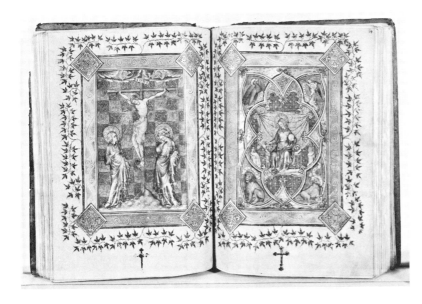

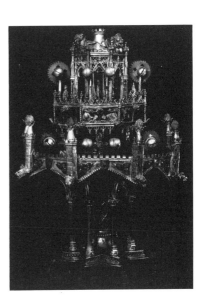

64

Three Mourners from the Tomb of Philip the Bold.
Vizelle alabaster (Grenoble stone).
Early 15th century. Claus Sluter and Claus de Werve,
Franco-Netherlandish. 40.128, 58.66, 58.67*

Leopard d'Or, Edward III. Gold.
Anglo-Gallic issue as King of
Aquitaine, third issue with English
and French titles, 1360. 64.373

Mouton d'Or, Jean le Bon.
Gold. France, 1350-1364. 64.372

Madonna and Child. Painted limestone
France, Central Loire Valley,
ca. 1385-1390. 62.28*

Triptych: Madonna and Child with Scenes of Annunciation, Visitation, Adoration. Ivory with gilding. France, late 14th century. 51.450

Madonna and Child from Mariapfarr in Lungau. Cast stone. Austria, Diocese of Salzburg, ca. 1395. 65.236*

The Coronation of the Virgin. Tempera on wood. The Rubielos Master, Spanish, Valencia, active ca. 1400. 47.208

Half of a Chasuble. Textile: velvet weave, silk; Italy, 15th century. Orphreys: embroidery, silk and gold on linen; Austria (Bohemia), 15th century. 50.85

Madonna and Child. Painted lindenwood. Upper Austria, Diocese of Passau, ca. 1370-1380. 62.207

Triptych (House Altar). Tempera on oak. Ca. 1425. Austrian Master. 41.68

Diptych: Four Scenes from the Passion. Tempera and oil on linen over oak(?). Austria, ca. 1400. 45.115

Coronation of the Virgin. Tempera on wood. Ca. 1410-1420. Master of the Frondenberg Altarpiece, German, Westphalia. 29.920

John the Baptist. Oak panel. Before 1425. Robert Campin (Master of Flémalle), Flemish. 66.238

The Death of the Virgin. Tempera on fir. First decade 15th century. Master of Heiligenkreuz, Austrian. 36.496*

Leaf from a Missal: Frontispiece for the Canon of the Mass. Tempera and gold leaf on vellum. North Netherlands, Guelders-Overijssel, Cloister Agnietenberg near Zwolle, ca. 1438-1439. Miniature painted by Master of Otto von Moerdrecht. 59.254

The Passion of Christ. Oil on wood. Master of the Schlägl Altarpiece, German, Westphalia, active 1440-1450. 51.453

Adoration of the Magi.
Tempera on fir. Konrad Laib, Austrian, Salzburg, active mid-15th century. 36.18

Virgin Weeping. Wood. Veit Stoss, German, 1447-ca. 1533. 39.64

A Bridal Pair. Tempera on fir. South Germany, Swabian School, ca. 1470. 32.179*

Four Gospels: fol. 2v, St. Matthew.
Vellum, Latin written in black,
illuminated with tempera and
gold leaf. Germany, Middle Rhine,
ca. 1480. Miniatures by the Master
of the Hausbuch. Contemporary
blind-stamped leather binding. 52.465*

Gothic Ornament of Oak-leaf Design.
Engraving. Master W with a Key,
Netherlandish, active ca. 1470. 52.100

Madonna and Child with Saints. Tapestry, wool, silk and linen.
Germany, Nuremberg, Franconia, 15th century. 39.162

The Adoration of the Magi.
Oil on oak. Geertgen Tot Sint Jans,
Dutch, ca. 1460-late 1480's. 51.353

The Crucifixion. Oil on oak.
Flanders, close to the Master of the
Sforza Triptych, ca. 1470. 31.449

Nativity. Oil on oak. Gerard David,
Flemish, 1450/60-1523. 58.320*

The Annunciation. Oil on oak.
Aelbrecht Bouts, Flemish,
ca. 1452/55-1549. 42.635

Hours of Ferdinand V and Isabella of Spain: fol. 126v, The Nativity.
Latin written in red and dark brown on vellum, illuminated in tempera and
gold. Flanders, Ghent-Bruges School, ca. 1492-1504. Miniatures by
Alexander Bening and Gerard Horenbout. 63.256*

A Monk Praying. Oil on oak.
Flanders, early 16th century. 42.632

Madonna and Child. Oil on oak.
Follower of Hans Memling, Flemish,
15th century. 34.29

St. John the Baptist.
Oil grisaille on oak. Dirk Bouts,
Dutch, ca. 1415-1475. 51.354

St. Andrew. Oak, traces of paint.
Netherlands, 15th century. 38.169

An Angel Supporting Two Escutcheons. Black chalk on pink-tinted paper.
Germany, Circle of Nicolaus Gerhaert von Leyden, ca. 1470. 62.205

Design for a Gothic Table Fountain.
Engraving. Master W with a Key,
Netherlandish, active ca. 1470. 37.565

Monstrance with Relic of St. Sebastian
From the Guelph Treasure.
Silver gilt and crystal. Germany,
Brunswick, ca. 1475. 31.65

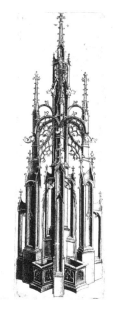

71

Abbot's Stall. Oak.
France, 1500-1515. 28.657

Madonna and Child. Oil on oak.
Cornelius van Coninxloo, Flemish,
active 1526-1558. 46.282

Double Mazer. Maple wood with
silver-gilt mounts. Germany, ca. 1530.
With portrait medallion (1528) of
Albrecht Dürer by Matthes Gebel,
Nuremburg and Augsburg. 50.83

Chest. Painted wood. Spain, Catalan(?), late 15th century. 228.15

The Flight into Egypt.
Engraving. Martin Schongauer,
German, before 1440-1491. 54.260

Story of Perseus and Andromeda. Tapestry, wool and silk. Flanders,
Tournai, ca. 1480. 161.27

Flight into Egypt. Tapestry, wool, silk, and gold. Flanders
Tournai, ca. 1480. 42.826

Plate: Inscribed: Maria. Majolica.
Spain, Valencia, Hispano-Moresque,
mid-15th century. 44.292

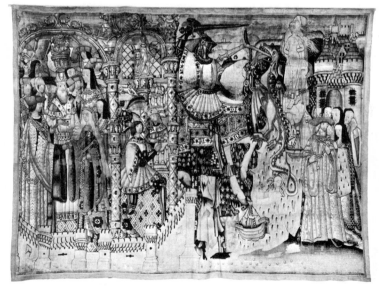

73

The *Annunciation*. Tempera on wood. Jaime Ferrer II, Spanish, active mid-15th century. 53.660

Portrait of a Lady. Oil on wood. Flanders, ca. 1480. 62.259

Holy Trinity. Oil on poplar. France, ca. 1465-1475. 60.79

Portrait Heads of a Man and Woman. Marble. France, Circle of Michel Colombe, early 16th century. 21.1003, 21.1004

Portrait of a Nobleman. Tempera and oil on oak. France, Burgundian, ca. 1480-1500. 63.503

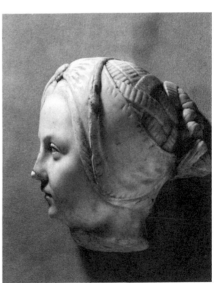

Mourner from the Tomb of Duke John the Fearless. Vizelle alabaster (Grenoble stone). Ca. 1462. Antoine le Moiturier, French. 40.129

Single Miniature from a Boccaccio, Des Cleres et Noble Femmes (now Spencer Ms. 33, New York Public Library): *Queen Medusa Enthroned.* Tempera and gold leaf on vellum. France, close to Maitre Francois, ca. 1470. 24.1015

Education of the Virgin. Stone. France, Bourbonnais, close to Jean de Chartres, early 16th century. 23.51

Triumph of Eternity. Tapestry, wool and silk. France, Valley of Loire, 1500-1510. 60.176*

75

Triptych. Onyx cameo: Italy, 13th century. Gold and translucent enamel: France, late 15th century. 47.508*

Youth. Tapestry, wool and silk. France, Valley of Loire, 1500-1510. 60.177

Lady with Three Suitors. Pen and brown ink and ink wash. France, 1490-1500. 56.40

Time. Tapestry, wool and silk. France, Valley of Loire, 1500-1510. 60.178

76

Christ Carrying His Cross. Engraving. Martin Schongauer, German, before 1440-1491. 41.389*

St. Lawrence and St. Stephen. Lindenwood. 1502-1510. Tilmann Riemenschneider, German. 59.42, 59.43*

Pietà. Painted lindenwood. Ca. 1515. Master of Rabenden, German, Bavaria. 38.294

Playing Card with King and Helmet.
Engraving. Master E.S., German,
active ca. 1450-1470. 49.564

*St. John the Baptist Surrounded by
the Evangelists and Four Fathers of
the Latin Church.* Dated 1466.
Engraving, state I/II. Master E.S.,
German. 50.585*

St. Jerome. Dotted print colored by
hand, state II/III. Germany,
ca. 1470-1475. 52.13

St. Jerome and the Lion. Alabaster.
Ca. 1510. Tilmann Riemenschneider,
German. 46.82*

*Head of a Man, an Angel, and
Two Small Profile Heads.*
Silverpoint heightened with white,
on prepared rose paper. Circle of
Benozzo Gozzoli, Italian,
1420-1497. 37.24*

Oak-leaf Jar. Majolica.
Italy, Florence,
2nd quarter 15th century. 43.54

Madonna and Child.
Glazed terra cotta. Ca. 1460-1470.
Luca della Robbia, Italian. 42.782

Portrait of a Man. Oil on walnut.
Colantonio del Fiore(?), Italian,
active in Naples
ca. 1430/40-1460/70. 16.811

Madonna and Child with Angels.
Tempera on poplar. Italy, Florence,
School of Fra Filippo Lippi,
ca. 1460-1470. 16.802

The Funeral of St. Stephen.
Pen and bistre ink. Fra Filippo Lippi,
Italian, 1406-1469. 47.70*

St. Michael and St. Anthony Abbot. Tempera on poplar. 1457-1458.
Fra Filippo Lippi, Italian, Florence. 64.150, 64.151*

Head of a Singing Boy. Marble.
Luca della Robbia, Italian,
Florence, 1400-1482. 31.454

80

Book Cover. Silver and niello.
Italy, Florence, ca. 1467-1469. 52.109*

Madonna and Child.
Tempera on poplar. Italy, Florence,
School of Alesso Baldovinetti,
ca. 1465. 16.789

Textile (detail). Diasper weave,
silk, linen, and gold.
Italy (Lucca?), 15th century. 31.61

Madonna and Child.
Silverpoint on rose prepared paper.
Lorenzo di Credi,
Italian, 1459/60-1537. 63.472

*Life of the Virgin and of Christ:
The Agony in the Garden.*
Engraving, state I/III. Italy,
Florence, ca. 1470-1490. 49.540

Madonna and Child.
Terra cotta. Ca. 1478.
Antonio Rossellino, Italian. 42.780

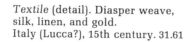

Page from a Prayer Book.
Tempera and gold leaf on vellum.
Attavante degli Attavanti,
Italian, Florence, 1452-1517. 53.280

Christ Child. Marble.
Baccio da Montelupo,
Italian, ca. 1469-1533. 42.799

Bust of Christ. Painted terra cotta.
Italy, Florence,
late 15th century. 21.956

The Last Supper. Engraving. Lucantonio degli Uberti,
Italian, 1495-1520. 40.473-a

St. Jerome in Penitence. Engraving. Italy, Florence, ca. 1480-1500. 49.33

St. John. Terra cotta. Master of the Statuettes of St. John, Italian, late 15th century. 42.781

Single Leaf: Adoration of the Shepherds. Tempera and gold leaf on vellum. Italy, Siena, style nearest to Guidoccio Cozzarelli or Matteo Giovanni, ca. 1470. 52.282

Paneling from a Sacristry Bench. Walnut, inlaid with holly and ebony. Italy, Florence, late 15th century. 193.15

83

The Crucifixion. Tempera on poplar. Matteo di Giovanni di Bartolo, Italian, Siena, 1430(?)-1495. 40.535

Leaf from a Gradual with Initial M. Tempera and gold leaf on vellum. Attributed to Cosimo Tura, Italian, Ferrarese School, 1432-1495. 27.425

Single Miniature: Christ on the Mount of Olives. Tempera on vellum. 1490-1500. Attributed to Timoteo Viti, Italian, Umbria. 27.161

The Lamentation. Tapestry, wool, silk, gold, and silver. Italy, Ferrara, after design by Cosimo Tura, ca. 1475. 50.145

St. Sebastian. Brush and brown ink over silverpoint on pink prepared paper. Pietro Perugino, Italian, 1445/50-1523. 58.411*

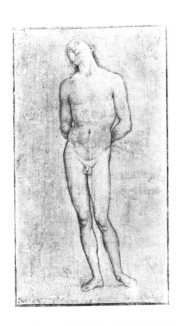

Drug Bottle. Majolica.
Italy, Faenza, ca. 1480. 43.52

Madonna and Child with St. Anthony Abbot, St. Sebastian, St. Mark, and St. Severino. Tempera on poplar.
Lorenzo d'Alessandro da San Severino, Italian,
active 1468-1503. 16.800

Holy Family with a Shepherd.
Oil on canvas. Dosso Dossi,
Italian, Ferrara, 1479(?)-1542. 49.185

Choral Book: Angel (detail).
Tempera and gold leaf on vellum.
Antonio Liberale da Verona, Italian,
1445-ca. 1526. 30.661

Adoration of the Christ Child.
Marble with some gilding. Italy,
Lombardy, late 15th century. 1874.28

85

Jar with Portrait. Majolica. Italy,
Caffaggiolo, ca. 1475-1480. 41.550

*The Adoration of the Magi, the
Virgin in the Grotto.* Engraving. Italy,
Mantegna School, after 1463. 54.66

Single Miniature: The Nativity.
Tempera and gold on vellum.
Girolamo dai Libri, Italian,
Verona, 1474-1555. 53.281

Virgin and Child. Marble.
Bartolommeo Bellano, Italian,
Padua, 1435-1496/97. 20.273

Plate. Majolica. Italy, Caffaggiolo,
late 15th century. 23.915

Mother and Child with Two Dogs.
Engraving. Italy,
late 15th century. 37.566

86

Adoration of the Magi. Bronze. Ca. 1500. Andrea Briosco (called Riccio), Italian, Padua. 54.601

Farm on the Slope of a Hill. Pen and brown ink. Fra Bartolommeo, Italian, 1472-1517. 57.498*

Pietà. Tempera on vellum. Attributed to Andrea Mantegna, Italian, Padua, 1431-1506. 51.394

Hercules and Antaeus. Engraving. Italy, Mantegna School, 15th century. 64.32

St. Christopher. Pen and brown ink with blue and green washes, touches of white. Andrea Mantegna, Italian, 1431-1506. 56.39*

Base for Satyr and Satyress Group. Bronze. Andrea Briosco (called Riccio), Italian, Padua, ca. 1470/75-1532. 50.375

Pomona. Bronze. Andrea Briosco (called Riccio), Italian, Padua, ca. 1470/75-1532. 48.486

Satyress. Bronze, 1510-1530. Andrea Briosco (called Riccio), Italian, Padua. 47.29*

Battle in a Wood. Engraving. Master of the Year 1515, Italian. 49.34

St. Nicholas of Bari.
Tempera on poplar.
Carlo Giovanni Crivelli, Italian,
Venice, ca. 1430/35-ca. 1495. 52.111

Portrait of a Youth. Oil on tempered
pressed wood. Bartolommeo Veneto,
Italian, Lombard-Venetian, active
1502-after 1530. 40.539

The Virgin and Child with St. Anthony Abbot, St. Lucy(?), and Two Donors.
Oil on tempered pressed wood. Cima da Conegliano, Italian, Venice,
1459/60-1517/18. 42.636

Marriage Beaker.
Enameled milk glass. Italy,
late 15th century. 55.70

Tarocchi Cards (E Series): Music.
Engraving, touched with gold. Italy,
Ferrara, not later than 1467. 24.457

Pedlar Goblet. Enameled
emerald green and blue glass.
Italy, ca. 1475. 53.364

Albarello. Majolica. Italy, Faenza,
early 16th century. 40.12

Bust of a Woman. Engraving.
Jacopo de' Barbari, Italian,
ca. 1450-before 1516. 32.38

Plate: The Prodigal Son, after Dürer.
Dated 1528. Majolica. Maestro Giorgio,
Italian, Faenza(?). 50.82

Ewer. Painted enamel.
Italy, Venice, ca. 1500. 23.720

Bird's-eye View of Venice (detail). Dated 1500. Woodcut, state I/III. Jacopo de' Barbari, Italian. 49.569

Textile (detail). Velvet weave, silk and gold. Italy, Venice. late 15th century. 31.63

Plate: The Three Graces. Majolica. 1525. Maestro Giorgio (Giorgio Andreoli da Gubbio), Italian, Gubbio. 45.2*

Textile. Velvet weave, silk. Italy, Venice, 15th century. 40.370

Man with an Arrow. Engraving, state II/II. Benedetto Montagna, Italian, ca. 1470-after 1540. 43.65

91

Venus Prudentia(?). Gilt bronze.
Italy, 1st half 16th century. 48.171

The Assumption of the Virgin.
Engraving, state I/II. Italy,
Florence, ca. 1490. 49.32*

Madonna and Child. From the
Ciborium of Cardinal d'Estouteville
in S. Maria Maggiore, Rome. Marble
relief. Ca. 1460. Mino del Reamè or
del Regno, Italian, Rome. 28.747*

Plate. Majolica. Italy, Deruta,
early 16th century. 23.1096

*The Holy Family with St. Margaret
and St. John.* Oil and tempera on
poplar. Filippino Lippi, Italian,
Florence, ca. 1457-1504. 32.227*

Figure of Plenty. Glazed terra cotta.
1520-1530. Giovanni della Robbia
(or his atelier), Italian, Florence. 40.343

Study for the Nude Youth over the Prophet Daniel, in the Sistine Chapel Ceiling Fresco. Red chalk. Michelangelo Buonarroti, Italian, 1475-1564. 40.465

Standing Figure of a Man. Bronze. Italy, Florence, mid-16th century. 47.509

Sacrifice of Isaac. Oil and tempera on poplar. Ca. 1525-1530. Andrea del Sarto, Italian, Florence. 37.577*

Plate: Sacrifice. Dated 1526. Signed: M. G. da Agubio. Majolica. Maestro Giorgio, Italian, Castel Durante(?). 50.156

Circular Table. Walnut. Italy, Florence, late 16th century. 39.183

93

Tazza with Putti Frieze.
Enameled blue glass. Italy,
Venice, ca. 1490. 60.38*

Venus Reclining in a Landscape. Engraving, state I/II. Giulio Campagnola,
Italian, ca. 1482-after 1515. 31.205*

The Fate of the Evil Tongue.
Engraving. Nicoletto Rosex
(da Modena), Italian, active
ca. 1490-after 1511. 47.11

Running Woman (Atalanta?). Bronze.
Maffeo Olivieri, Italian,
Brescia, 1484-1543/44. 63.92

Venus. Bronze. Ca. 1560.
Danese Cattaneo, Italian, active in
Venice and the Veneto, 1509-1573. 50.578

Adoration of the Magi. Oil on canvas. Ca. 1560. Titian, Italian, Venice. 57.150

Baptism of Christ. Oil on canvas. After 1580.
Tintoretto (Jacopo Robusti), Italian, Venice. 50.400*

Madonna and Child.
Signed: Iacobus Sansovo. Bronze.
Jacopo Tatti (called Sansovino),
Italian, Florence 1486-
Venice 1570. 51.316*

St. John the Baptist. Bronze.
Jacopo Tatti (called Sansovino),
Italian, Florence 1486-
Venice 1570. 52.276

Albarello: Andromeda Saved by Perseus. Majolica. Italy, Venice, Workshop of Domenigo da Venezia, early 16th century. 20.421

St. Margaret. Marble. 1520-1530. Antonello Gagini, Italian, Sicilian School. 42.564

The Assumption of the Virgin. Dated 1517. Engraving, state I/II. Domenico Campagnola, Italian. 54.741

Virgin and Child Enthroned. Verre églomise. Italy, 16th century. *Frame:* Silver and enamel. Germany, Augsburg, ca. 1600. 53.284

Pendant: Madonna and Child with Saints. Enameled gold with pearls and emeralds. Italy, late 16th century. 59.337*

The Dead Christ With Joseph of Arimathea. Oil on poplar. Ca. 1525. Giovanni Girolamo Savoldo, Italian, Brescia. 52.512

Portrait of a Gentleman and His Wife. Oil on canvas. Italo-Flemish, 16th century. 16.793

Portrait of Vincenzo Guarignoni. Dated 1572. Oil on canvas. Giovanni Battista Moroni, Italian, Brescia. 62.1

Credenza. Walnut. Italy, Brescia, mid-16th century. 39.188

Portrait of a Nobleman.
Oil on canvas. 1525. Lorenzo Lotto,
Italian, Venice. 50.250

Portrait of Agostino Barbarigo.
Oil on canvas. Ca. 1570.
Paolo Veronese, Italian, Venice 28.16

Head of St. John the Baptist. Oil on canvas. Lorenzo Lotto,
Italian, Venice, 1480-1556. 53.424

Cassone Frontal. Walnut. Italy, 16th century. 236.15

Lazarus and the Rich Man. Oil on canvas. Ca. 1550. Jacopo Bassano, Italian. 39.68*

The Entombment. Oil on canvas. Ca. 1580. Leandro Bassano, Italian, Venice. 16.806

Annunciation. Oil on canvas. Paolo Veronese, Italian, Venice, 1528-1588. 50.251

Espalier Plates. Steel. Attributed to Negroli, Italian, Milan, 16th century. 16.1517, 16.1518

Annunciation. Pen and brown ink and gray wash. Luca Cambiaso, Italian, 1527-1585. 59.200

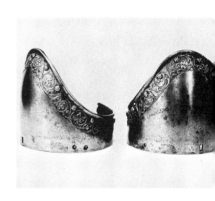

Apollo on Parnassus, Surrounded by Muses and Poets. Engraving, before state I/II. Marcantonio Raimondi, Italian, ca. 1480-ca. 1530. 63.231

Cassone. Walnut. Italy, Venice, mid-16th century. 42.607

Plaque: Feast of the Gods. Bronze. Alessandro Vittoria, Italian, Trent 1525-Venice 1608. 52.464

Plate. Majolica. Italy, Urbino, Atelier of the Fontana Family, ca. 1560. 42.622

Mars. Bronze. Giovanni Bologna, Italian, Douai (Belgium) 1529-Florence 1608. 64.421*

Medici Plate. Soft paste porcelain. Italy, Florence, ca. 1580. 49.489

Study for Aeneas' Flight from Troy. Pen and brown ink, black chalk, brown and light yellow wash on gray-green paper. Federico Barocci, Italian, 1535(?)-1612. 60.26*

Dressoir. Walnut. France, Burgundy, mid-16th century. 42.606

The Apocalypse: St. John Sees the Four Riders. Engraving. Jean Duvet, French, 1485-after 1556. 53.222

Chest. Oak. France, Normandy, 2nd half 16th century. 42.604

Ewer with Relief Scenes of Allegorical Subjects. Silver gilt. Ca. 1580. Attributed to François Briot, French, Strasbourg. 40.16

Hat Jewel: The Rape of Helen. Enamel on gold. France, mid-16th century. 49.377*

Hat Jewel: Adoration of the Kings. Enamel on gold, France, ca. 1540. 38.428*

Portrait of a Princess. Oil on oak.
Corneille de Lyon, French,
ca. 1520-1574(?). 42.48

Mirror Back. Enamel "en resille."
France, 2nd half 16th century. 26.246

Two Allegorical Figures. Painted wood. France, Circle of
Francesco Primaticcio, ca. 1560. 59.345, 59.346

St. Porchaire Ewer. Faience.
France, 16th century. 53.363

103

Ewer Stand. Dated 1557.
Enamel on copper. Pierre Reymond,
French, Limoges. 40.139

*Seated Woman and Two Children
(Charity?).* Alabaster. Attributed to
Germain Pilon, French,
ca. 1535-1590. 51.541

Inlaid Table. Walnut. France, Burgundian School, 2nd half 16th century. 42.601

St. Porchaire Pedestal Dish. Faience.
France, 16th century. 52.278

Samson and Delilah. Woodcut.
Lucas van Leyden, Dutch,
1494-1533. 35.117

Adoration of the Shepherds.
Engraving. Frans Crabbe, Flemish,
ca. 1480-1553. 66.121

Return of the Prodigal Son. Engraving. Lucas van Leyden,
Dutch, 1494-1533. 27.361

Landscape with Venus and Adonis. Oil on copper. Gillis van Coninxloo,
Flemish, 1544-1606/07. 62.293

Two Peasants in Half Figure.
Pen and light brown ink over
black chalk. Pieter Bruegel I,
Flemish, 1525-1569. 45.114

*The Apocalypse: The Riders on the
Four Horses.* Woodcut.
Albrecht Dürer, German,
1471-1528. 32.313

Portrait of an Elizabethan Gallant.
Dated 1576. On vellum.
Nicholas Hilliard, English. 60.39

Sir Anthony Mildmay.
Water color on vellum.
Nicholas Hilliard,
English, 1547(?)-1619. 26.554*

The Dead Christ. Dated 1505. Charcoal. Albrecht Dürer, German. 52.531*

The Arm of Eve. Dated 1507.
Brush drawing in brown and white
ink on blue paper. Albrecht Dürer,
German. 65.470*

Adam and Eve. Bronze. Germany,
Nuremberg, Circle of Peter Vischer,
the Younger, ca. 1520. 61.29

Adam and Eve. Dated 1515. Bronze.
Ludwig Krug, German,
Nuremberg, 48.359

Adam and Eve. Boxwood. Attributed to Conrad Meit, South German,
1470/80-ca. 1550. 46.429, 46.491*

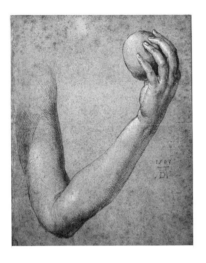

The Virgin with a Monkey.
Engraving. Albrecht Dürer,
German, 1471-1528. 64.29

*Plaque: Christ in the Garden of
Gethsemane.* Kelheim stone.
Attributed to Adolph Daucher,
German, Augsburg, d. ca. 1523. 47.182

Adoration of the Shepherds. Oil on
wood. 1st half 16th century. Master
of the Ansbach Kelterbild (perhaps
Hans Springinklee), German. 16.807

The Ascension. Pen and brown ink.
Albrecht Dürer, German 1471-1528.
52.530

The Virgin on the Crescent Moon.
Woodcut, proof before text.
Albrecht Dürer, German, 1471-1528.
59.99

Christ on the Mount of Olives.
Dated 1515. Etching on iron.
Albrecht Dürer, German. 43.389

Medal: The Trinity. Dated 1544.
Silver. Hans Reinhart the Elder,
German. 56.337

The Stag Hunt. Dated 1540. Oil on wood. Lucas Cranach the Elder with
assistance of Lucas Cranach the Younger, German. 58.425

The Organ Player and His Wife.
Engraving, state I/III. Israhel van
Meckenem, German, before
1450-1503. 60.73

Sitting Dog Scratching Himself.
Bronze. Germany, Nuremberg,
2nd quarter 16th century. 60.74

Model for Equestrian Monument of Emperor Maximilian. Bronze.
Gregor Erhart, German, ca. 1470-1540/41. 52.108

*Equestrian Portrait of the
Emperor Maximilian.* Dated 1508.
Woodcut printed from two outline
blocks on blue hand-tinted paper.
Hans Burgkmair, German. 50.72*

Armet, Helmet in Maximilian Style.
Steel. Germany,
early 16th century. 16.1855

The Bewitched Groom. Woodcut.
1544. Hans Baldung (called Grien),
German. 66.172

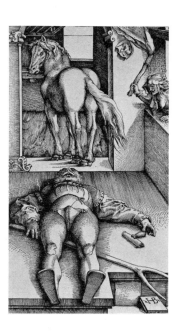

Mass of St. Gregory. Oil on wood. Hans Baldung (called Grien), German, ca. 1480-1545. 52.112*

Pyramus and Thisbe. Chiaroscuro woodcut. Hans Wechtlin, German, 1480/85-after 1526. 50.396

Der Weisskunig: The Banished Duke of Otnop. Woodcut. Hans Burgkmair, German, 1473-1531. 60.28

Crucifix. Lindenwood. Ca. 1525-1530. Hans Lainberger, German, Bavaria. 38.293

Portrait Medallion. Boxwood. Attributed to Friedrich Hagenauer, South German, active 1527-1546. 27.42

111

Portrait Plaque of Georg Knauer.
Pearwood. Peter Dell, South German,
1501-1545(?). 27.427*

Pendant with Pelican.
Enameled gold with rubies.
Germany, ca. 1600. 59.336

*Portrait of Maria von Kitscher, Frau
Pancraz von Freyberg zu Aschau.*
Dated 1545. Oil on lindenwood.
Hans Mielich, German. 44.88

Model for Medal: Pope Alexander V.
Kelheim stone. Tobias Wolff,
German, Breslau, d. ca. 1570. 56.28

Sir Thomas More. Oil on wood.
Hans Holbein the Younger,
German, 1497/98-1543/44. 57.356

*Model for Medal: Son of Martin III
Geuder.* Kelheim stone. Matthes Gebel,
German, Nuremberg, ca. 1500-1574. 56.25

Salome with the Head of St. John the Baptist. Pen and brush in black ink heightened with white on brown tinted paper. Albrecht Altdorfer, German, ca. 1480-1538. 48.440*

View of a Castle. Dated 1513. Pen and bistre ink. Wolfgang Huber, Austrian. 51.277

The Fall and Redemption of Man: Four Scenes from the Passion of Christ. Four woodcuts printed on one page. Albrecht Altdorfer, German, ca. 1480-1538. 52.50-52.53

The Visitation. Oil on wood. Ca. 1520. Bavarian or Austrian Master of the Danube School (perhaps Master "I"). 50.91

Standing Cup with Cover. Silver gilt. Germany, Nuremberg, 2nd half 16th century. 62.226

113

River Landscape with Five Bare Spruce Trees in the Foreground.
Dated 1549. Etching. Augustin Hirschvogel, German. 51.491

Scales. Gilt bronze. Germany,
Nuremberg, Jamnitzer Workshop,
ca. 1565-1570. 50.382*

Faience Owl. Dated 1540.
South Germany. 50.370

Mortar. Bronze. Germany,
Nuremberg, 1st half 16th century.
Plaquettes by Peter Flötner, 51.444

*Sextus Tarquinius Threatening
Lucrece.* Bronze. Hubert Gerhard,
German, ca. 1540/50-1620. 62.245*

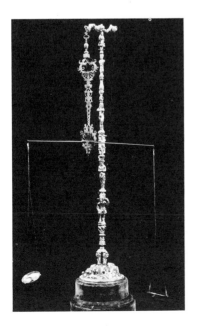

Allegory of Christian Belief.
Dated 162(2?). Pen and bistre ink
and bistre wash. Johann Liss,
German, Venetian School. 53.6

Minerva. Oil on canvas.
Bernard Strozzi, Italian,
Genoese-Venetian, 1581-1644. 29.133

St. Sebastian. Bronze. 17th century.
Follower of Pietro Tacca, perhaps
Georg Petel, Italian. 40.585

Pietà. Oil on canvas. Bernardo Strozzi, Italian, Genoese-Venetian,
1581-1644. 53.27

Study for Minerva. Black and red chalk. Bernardo Strozzi, Italian, Genoese-Venetian, 1581-1644. 53.626

Pope Innocent X. Bronze. Alessandro Algardi and assistants, Italian, Rome, 1595-1654. 57.496

Venus and Cupid. Pen and bistre ink and bistre wash with red chalk indications. Giovanni Francesco Barbieri (called Guercino), Italian, 1591-1666. 25.1188*

St. Jerome. Oil on canvas. Giovanni Battista Langetti, Italian, Genoese-Venetian, 1625-1676. 51.334

The Feast of Terminus. Drawing in red-brown oil. Giovanni Benedetto Castiglione, Italian, 1616-1670. 64.31

116

The Blessed Alessandro Sauli. Terra cotta. Pierre Puget, French, active in Italy, 1620-1694. 64.36*

Landscape with Nymphs and Satyrs. Oil on canvas. Nicolas Poussin (?), French, 1594-1665. 26.26

The Apparition of the Virgin to St. Francis of Assisi. Oil on canvas. Ca. 1680-1683. Luca Giordano, Italian, Naples. 66.125

Endymion. Marble. Agostino Cornacchini, Italian, 1685-1740. 42.51

Return to Nazareth. Oil on canvas. Nicolas Poussin, French, 1594-1665. 53.156

Italian Landscape. Pen and brush and brown ink. Nicolas Poussin, French, 1594-1665. 58.421

L'Impruneta (first plate). Dated 1620. Etching, state III/VI. Jacques Callot, French. 62.20

The Martyrdom of St. Lucy. Etching, state II/II. Jacques Bell'ange, French, 1594-1638. 50.214

The Repentant St. Peter. Dated 1645. Oil on canvas. Georges de La Tour, French, 51.454*

Roman Campagna near Tivoli. Dated 163(?). Oil on canvas. Claude Gellée (called Claude Lorrain), French. 46.73

Landscape with Cattle. Pen and brown ink and ink wash. Claude Gellée (called Claude Lorrain), French, 1600-1682. 28.15*

Landscape with Rest on the Flight into Egypt. Oil on canvas. Claude Gellée (called Claude Lorrain), French, 1600-1682. 62.151*

Charles II, King of England. Dated 1653. Oil on canvas. Philippe de Champaigne, French. 59.3

Dance of the Boys and Girls. Oil on canvas. Mathieu Le Nain, French, ca. 1607-1677. 57.489

Diana and Her Nymphs Departing for the Chase. Oil on canvas. Ca. 1615. Peter Paul Rubens, Flemish. 59.190*

Portrait of Isabella Brant. Oil on wood. Ca. 1620-1622. Peter Paul Rubens, Flemish, 47.207*

Jar. Soft paste porcelain. France, Rouen, Poterat Factory(?), ca. 1680. 47.63

The Feast of Herod. Pen and bistre ink with charcoal and red chalk. Peter Paul Rubens, Flemish, 1577-1640. 54.2*

A Genoese Lady with Her Child.
Oil on canvas. Ca. 1621-1627. Sir
Anthony van Dyck, Flemish. 54.392

*The Conversion of St. Paul with
Horseman and Banner.* Ink, black and
red chalk, and water color. Jacob
Jordaens, Flemish, 1593-1678. 54.366*

Portrait of Frans Snyders. Etching,
state I/IV. Sir Anthony van Dyck,
Flemish, 1599-1641. 42.741

Boar Hunt. Brush with black and gray ink heightened with white. Jan Fyt,
Flemish, 1611-1661. 60.157

The Lamentation. Black chalk and ink
heightened with white. Sir Anthony
van Dyck, Flemish, 1599-1641. 66.174

Game of Backgammon. Oil on canvas. David Teniers the Younger,
Flemish, 1610-1690. 43.377

Peasants Drinking and Smoking.
Oil on oak. David Teniers the   *Hollow Tree.* Pen and ink and water color. Roeland Savery,
Younger, Flemish, 1610-1690. 16.1046   Dutch. 1576-1639. 58.315

View of Orleans on the Loire. Pen and brown ink, brown and gray wash. Lambert Doomer, Dutch, 1622/23-1700. 66.4

A View of Emmerich across the Rhine. Dated 1645. Oil on oak. Jan van Goyen, Dutch. 59.351*

Hilly Landscape with Hut beside a Stream. Dated 1627. Black chalk and tan and gray wash. Esaias van de Velde, Dutch. 66.7

Landscape with a Cottage and Figures. Dated 1653. Pencil and gray wash. Jan van Goyen, Dutch. 29.548

Portrait of a Lady in a Ruff.
Dated 1638. Oil on canvas.
Frans Hals, Dutch. 48.137*

Portrait of a Youth. Dated 1632.
Oil on oak. Rembrandt Harmensz
van Rijn, Dutch. 42.644

Portrait of a Lady. Dated 1635.
Oil on oak. Rembrandt Harmensz
van Rijn, Dutch. 44.90

Christ Taken before Caiaphas. Pen, reed pen, and brush
with bistre ink and touches of white. Rembrandt
Harmensz van Rijn, Dutch, 1606-1669. 60.187

Christ Preaching (La Petite Tombe). Etching.
Rembrandt Harmensz van Rijn, Dutch, 1606-1669. 58.306

Portrait of a Young Student.
Oil on canvas. Rembrandt Harmensz
van Rijn, Dutch, 1606-1669. 50.252

The Three Crosses. Dated 1653. Etching and drypoint,
state IV/V. Rembrandt Harmensz van Rijn, Dutch. 59.241

The Meeting of Christ with Martha and Mary after the Death of Lazarus.
Reed pen and bistre with touches of white. Rembrandt Hermensz van Rijn,
Dutch, 1606-1669. 62.116*

Esther, Ahasuerus, and Haman. Oil on canvas. Jan Steen,
Dutch, 1626-1679. 64.153*

125

Mountainous Landscape. Pencil and ink. Nicolas Berchem, Dutch, 1620-1683. 58.410

Still Life. Dated 1663. Oil on canvas. Willem Kalf, Dutch. 62.292*

A Wooded and Hilly Landscape. Oil on canvas. Jacob van Ruisdael, Dutch, ca. 1628/29-1682. 63.575*

Portrait of a Standing Lady.
Oil on canvas. Gerard Terborch,
Dutch, 1617-1681. 44.93

Landscape with Canal. Oil on board. Jan Wijnants, Dutch, 1615/25-1682. 64.419

The Music Party. Oil on canvas. Pieter de Hooch,
Dutch, 1629-ca. 1683. 51.355

A Wooded Landscape with Figures. Oil on canvas.
Meindert Hobbema, Dutch, 1638-1709. 42.641

Travelers in a Hilly Landscape with a River. Oil on oak. Aelbert Cuyp, Dutch, 1620-1691. 42.637

Portrait of a Man. Oil on canvas. England, 17th century. 46.161

Thomas Hobbes. On vellum. Ca. 1660. Samuel Cooper, English. 49.548

Portrait of a Lady of the Earle Family. Oil on canvas. Sir Peter Lely, English, 1618-1680. 42.247

Mirror Frame (detail). Embroidery (stump work), silk and metal threads on satin. England, 17th century. 42.833

128

Spoon. Silver. 1661. John Hull and
Robert Sanderson. American,
Boston. 40.214

Covered Cup. Silver and silver gilt.
1677-1678. I.A. (unidentified),
English, London. 58.422

Armchair. Walnut with carved back.
England, ca. 1680-85. 42.573

Goblet. Engraved glass. 1680.
Herman Schwinger, German,
Nuremberg. 50.389

Fragment of an Altar Frontal (detail).
Embroidery, petit point. England,
period of Charles I, 1625-1649. 19.585

Covered Cup. Silver. 1686-1687. W.I.
(unidentified), English, London. 35.145

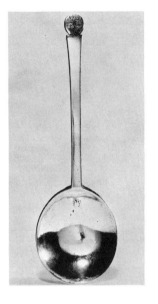

129

Covered Cup. Silver and silver gilt. 1688. Johann Andreas Thelot, German, Augsburg. 66.111

Vase. Red stoneware. Germany, Meissen, ca. 1708. 47.285

Flute. Engraved and cut glass. Germany, Thuringia, early 18th century. 51.545

Pilgrim Bottle. Polished stoneware with silver-gilt mounts. Germany, Meissen, ca. 1715. 51.451

Covered Goblet. Engraved glass. Bohemia, ca. 1715. 50.390

Knife, Fork, and Spoon. Gold. Germany, Augsburg, ca. 1725. 63.473-63.475

The Holy Family. Oil on canvas. El Greco (Domenikos Theotocopoulos), Spanish, ca. 1545-1614. 26.247*

Portrait of the Jester Calabazas. Oil on canvas. Ca. 1632. Diego Rodriguez de Silva y Velazquez, Spanish. 65.15*

Christ on the Cross with Landscape. Oil on canvas. El Greco (Domenikos Theotocopoulos), Spanish, ca. 1545-1614. 52.222

The Holy House of Nazareth. Oil on canvas. Francisco de Zurbarán, Spanish, 1598-1664. 60.117*

131

The Death of Adonis. Oil on canvas. 1635-1639. Jusepe de Ribera, Spanish. 65.19*

St. Jerome. Oil on canvas. Jusepe de Ribera, Spanish, ca. 1590-1652. 61.219

The Immaculate Conception. Oil on canvas. Bartolomé Estebán Murillo, Spanish, 1617-1682. 59.189

Laban Searching for His Stolen Household Gods in Jacob's Tent. Oil on canvas. 1665-70. Bartolomé Estebán Murillo, Spanish. 65.469*

132

Ebony Cabinet. Wood, metal, and tortoise shell. Attributed to André-Charles Boulle, French, Paris, 1642-1723. 49.539*

Mirror Frame. Gilded wood. France, ca. 1715. 53.153

Armchair. Oak. France, ca. 1715-1725. 25.1219

The Minuet in a Pavilion. Oil on canvas. Jean Antoine Watteau, French, 1684-1721. 38.392

Study for The Romancer. Red and black chalk. Jean Antoine Watteau, French, 1684-1721. 28.661

Seasons and Elements. Tapestry, silk and wool. France, Paris (Gobelin), 18th century. 42.495

The Declaration of Love. Oil on canvas. Nicolas Lancret, French, 1690-1743. 44.86

Spring. Savonnerie panel (knotted pile), silk and wool. France, Paris (Savonnerie), 18th century. 52.14

The Swing. Oil on canvas. Nicolas Lancret, French, 1690-1743. 48.180

Young St. John and the Lamb. Bronze. France, early 18th century. 40.586

Gaming Table. Wood and ivory marquetry. Italy, Piedmont(?), ca. 1730. 53.284

Cachepot. Soft paste porcelain. France, Paris, Villeroy Factory, ca. 1735-1740. 47.60

Seated Chinese with a Pot. Soft paste porcelain. France, Chantilly, ca. 1740. 47.62

Cachepot. Soft paste porcelain. France, St. Cloud, ca. 1725. 44.226

Portrait of Jean-Gabriel de la Porte du Theil. Oil on canvas. Ca. 1739/40. Jacques-André-Joseph-Camelot Aved, French. 64.89

Cupids in Conspiracy. Oil on canvas. François Boucher, French, 1703-1770. 48.182

The Flute Player. Tapestry, silk and wool. France, Beauvais, 18th century. 42.822

Chinese Fair. Tapestry, silk and wool. France, Beauvais, 18th century. 44.134*

The Fountain. Red, black, and white chalk. François Boucher, French, 1703-1770. 52.529

The Bagpipe Player. Soft paste biscuit porcelain. 1752-1753. After a design by François Boucher, French, Paris. Executed by Blondeau, French, Vincennes-Sèvres. 61.11

Mlle. de Savigny. Oil on canvas.
Ca. 1748. Jean Marc Nattier,
French. 48.183

Bust of a Woman. Terra cotta.
Jean Baptiste Lemoyne II,
French, 1704-1778. 52.566*

Madame de Pompadour as Diana.
Dated 1752. Oil on canvas. Jean Marc
Nattier, French. 42.643

Carpet. Wool. France, Paris (Savonnerie), ca. 1750. 50.8*

La Marquise d'Aiguirandes.
Dated 1759. Oil on canvas. François
Hubert Drouais, French. 42.638

Tall Clock (Regulateur). Tortoise shell and brass marquetry and ebony veneer with gilt-bronze mounts. 1744. Jacques-Pierre Latz, French, Paris. 49.200*

Candelabrum. Gilt bronze. Attributed to Jean Joseph de Saint-Germain, French, Paris, 1720-1791. 46.81*

Commode. Wood marquetry with gilt-bronze mounts. France, Paris, ca. 1750. 42.497

Gilt-bronze Clock. France, mid-18th century. 51.550

Wall Clock. Gilt bronze. France, mid-18th century. 50.376

Pair of Fire Dogs. Gilt bronze. 1752. Jacques Caffieri, French, Paris. 42.799, 42.800*

Candelabrum. Silver. 1758. François Thomas Germain, French, Paris. 40.14

Porcelain Vase. Germany, Meissen, 1749. *Gilt-bronze mounts:* France, Paris, mid-18th century. 44.230

Pair of Parrots. Porcelain. Ca. 1740. Modeled by Johann Joachim Kaendler, German, Meissen. *Pair of Candelabra.* Gilt bronze. France, Paris, mid-18th century. 38.305-38.308

Six Miniatures. Gouache on card.
1753. Louis Nicholas van
Blarenberghe, French.
Rectangular Box. Gold. 1753-1754.
Jean Charles Ducrollay, French,
Paris. 57.412

Laban Cherchant Ses Dieux. Oil on
canvas. Ca. 1753. Gabriel de Saint-
Aubin, French. 65.548

Fête in a Park with Costumed Dancers. Ink, ink and water-color washes,
over pencil indications. Ca. 1760-1765. Gabriel de Saint-Aubin, French. 66.124

Covered Bowl. Soft paste porcelain.
France, Vincennes, ca. 1745. 44.225

Tureen. Soft paste porcelain.
France, Vincennes, ca. 1752. 52.3*

Tureen. Soft paste porcelain. France, Vincennes-Sèvres, probably 1756. 49.15

Tureen with Platter. Soft paste porcelain. France, Sèvres, 1757. 53.25

Monkey on a Dog. Soft paste porcelain. France, Mennecy, mid-18th century. 53.269

Cachepot. Faience. France, Marseilles, Robert Factory, ca. 1765. 62.379

Covered Bowl. Faience. France, St. Clement, ca. 1775. 61.2

Morpheus. Oil on canvas. Jean Honoré Fragonard, French, 1732-1806. 63.502

Young Boy Dressed in a Red-lined Cloak (the Artist's Son?). Oil on canvas. Ca. 1789. Jean Honoré Fragonard, French. 42.49

Invocation to Love. Pen and brown ink and ink wash. Jean Honoré Fragonard, French, 1732-1806. 43.657*

Table-desk (Bureau plat). Wood marquetry with gilt-bronze mounts. Bernard van Risen Burgh II, French, Paris, active ca. 1730-1765/66. 44.123*

Table-desk. Wood marquetry with gilt-bronze mounts. Jacques Dubois, French, Paris, 1693-1763. 42.591

Straw Marquetry Desk. France, 3rd quarter 18th century. 42.40

The Synagogue. Oil on canvas. Alessandro Magnasco, Italian, Genoa, 1667-1749. 30.22*

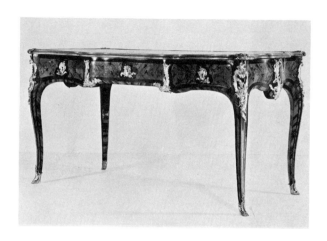

The Assumption of the Virgin.
Oil on canvas (modello). 1744.
Giovanni Battista Piazzetta,
Italian, Venice. 55.165

David and Goliath. Terra cotta. 1723.
Giovanni Battista Foggini, Italian,
Florentine. 66.126

The Supper at Emmaus. Oil on canvas.
Giovanni Battista Piazzetta, Italian,
Venice, 1682-1754. 31.245

Il fiorellin d'amore (Little Flower of Love). Black charcoal
heightened with white chalk. Giovanni Battista Piazzetta,
Italian, Venice, 1682-1754. 38.387*

Rest on the Flight into Egypt. Terra cotta.
Giuseppe Mazza, Italian, Bologna, 1653-1741. 64.427

Horatius Cocles Swimming the Tiber. Oil on canvas.
Giovanni Battista Tiepolo, Italian, Venice,
1696-1770. 49.572

Horatius Cocles Defending Rome against the Etruscans.
Oil on canvas. Giovanni Battista Tiepolo, Italian,
Venice, 1696-1770. 49.571

The Adoration of the Magi. Pen
and brush and bistre ink. Giovanni
Battista Tiepolo, Italian,
1696-1770. 44.474

Flight into Egypt: The Holy Family Embarking in a Small Boat. Pen and
bistre ink and bistre wash. Giovanni Battista Tiepolo, Italian, Venice,
1696-1770. 29.443*

Martyrdom of St. Sebastian: Modello for Diessen Altarpiece. Oil on canvas. Ca. 1739. Giovanni Battista Tiepolo, Italian, Venice. 46.277

Portrait of a Lady. Oil on canvas. Giovanni Battista Tiepolo, Italian, Venice, 1696-1770. 52.541

The Sacrifice of Isaac. Oil on canvas. Giovanni Antonio Guardi, Italian, Venice, 1698-1760. 52.235

The Angels Appearing to Abraham. Oil on canvas. Giovanni Antonio Guardi, Italian, Venice, 1698-1760. 52.237

Abraham Welcoming the Three Angels. Oil on canvas. Giovanni Antonio Guardi, Italian, Venice, 1698-1760. 52.238

View of the Piazza San Marco, Venice, and the Piazzetta Looking toward San Giorgio Maggiore. Oil on canvas. Giovanni Antonio Canale (called Canaletto), Italian, Venice, 1697-1768. 62.169*

Tobias and the Angel. Oil on canvas. Giovanni Antonio Guardi, Italian, Venice, 1698-1760. 52.236

Views of Venice and Environs: The Tower of Malghera. Etching, state I/II. Giovanni Antonio Canale (called Canaletto), Italian, Venice, 1697-1768. 25.1240

Woman and Man. Porcelain. Italy,
Naples, Capo-di-Monte,
mid-18th century. 50.569

Standing Woman. Porcelain. Italy,
Naples, Capo-di-Monte,
mid-18th century. 50.570

Imaginary View: A Palace on the Shore of the Lagoon. Pen and brown ink
with gray wash. Giovanni Antonio Canale (called Canaletto), Italian,
Venice, 1697-1768. 30.23*

Pietà. Oil on canvas. Giuseppe Bazzani, Italian, 1690-1769. 55.682

Visit of the Pope in Venice: The Pope Greets the Representatives of La Serenissima. Oil on canvas. 1782. Francesco Guardi, Italian, Venice. 49.187

A Procession of Triumphal Cars in Piazza S. Marco, Venice. Pen and bistre ink and bistre wash. 1782. Francesco Guardi, Italian, Venice. 55.164

Visit of the Pope in Venice: Pontifical Ceremony in the Church of SS. Giovanni e Paolo. Oil on canvas. 1782. Francesco Guardi, Italian, Venice. 49.188

The Spring Shower. Pen and bistre ink and bistre wash. Giovanni Domenico Tiepolo, Italian, Venice. 1727-1804. 37.573*

149

The Prisons: An Immense Interior with a Drawbridge, Etching, state I/III. Giovanni Battista Piranesi, Italian, 1720-1778. 41.30

God the Father. Painted and gilded wood. Johann Peter Schwanthaler the Elder, Austrian, 1720-1795. 61.30

House Altarpiece. Gilded wood. Circle of Georg Raphael Donner, Austrian, Vienna, 1693-1741. 64.357*

St. Joachim. Gilded wood. Joseph Anton Feuchtmeyer (or his circle), South German, 1696-1770. 62.246

Christ at the Column. Dated 1756. Gilt bronze. Johann Baptist Hagenauer, Austrian. 53.286*

Presentation of Christ in the Temple. Oil on canvas. Franz Anton Maulbertsch, Austrian, 1724-1796. 63.326

150

Kneeling Saint. Painted and gilded wood. Johann Baptist Straub, German, Munich, 1704-1784. 61.414

Putto. Painted and gilded wood. Workshop of Franz Ignaz Günther, German, Bavaria, 1725-1775. 61.413

Kneeling Angel. Carved wood. Ca. 1760. Franz Ignaz Günther, German, Bavaria, 1725-1775. 66.18

Spring. Painted and gilded wood. Ferdinand Tietz (or Dietz), Bohemia 1708—Germany, Franconia, 1777. 62.209

Madonna of the Immaculate Conception. Painted and gilded wood. Franz Ignaz Günther, German, Bavaria, 1725-1775. 63.294*

Console Table. Made for Schloss Seehof, Franconia. Gilded wood. Attributed to Ferdinand Tietz (or Dietz), Bohemia 1708—Germany, Franconia, 1777. 62.63

Harmony. Porcelain. Ca. 1740. Modeled by Johann Joachim Kaendler, German, Meissen. 50.79

Pluto. Porcelain. Ca. 1760. Modeled by Franz Anton Bustelli, German, Munich, Nymphenburg Factory. 47.283

Gilt-bronze Dish. Germany(?), 18th century. 55.69

Count Tschernitscheff, Russian Ambassador at Vienna. On ivory. Friedrich Heinrich Füger. German, 1751-1818. 42.1141

Tea Caddy. Silver gilt. 1741-42. Paul de Lamerie, English, London. 43.179

Punch Bowl. Soft paste porcelain. England, Worcester, ca. 1770. 38.331

Snuffer and Tray. Silver. John Burt, American, Boston, 1691-1745. 40.163, 40.164

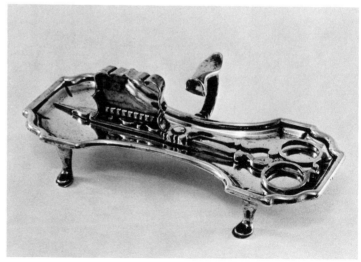

153

Teapot. Silver. Nathaniel Hurd, American, Boston, 1729-1777. 40.228*

Tankard. Silver. Edward Winslow, American, Boston, 1669-1753. 40.283

Brazier. Silver with wood handle and feet. John Potwine, American, Boston, 1698-1792. 40.248

154

The Ladies Amabel and Mary Jemima Yorke. Oil on canvas. 1761. Sir Joshua Reynolds, English. 42.645*

Scene with a Road Winding through a Wood. Pen and brown ink and gray wash. Thomas Gainsborough, English, 1727-1788. 29.547

Mrs. Thomas Samuel Joliffe. Oil on canvas. Gainsborough Dupont, English, 1754-1797. 42.640

Young Man in Blue. Dated 1778. On ivory. John Smart, English. 40.1219

A Storm behind the Isle of Wight. Oil on canvas. Julius Ibbetson, English, 1759-1817. 48.461

Portrait of Charles Apthorp.
Dated 1748. Oil on canvas. Robert Feke, American. 841.19

Portrait of Mrs. Theodore Atkinson.
Dated 1760. Oil on canvas.
Joseph Blackburn, American. 563.19

Portrait of Mrs. Thomas Bulfinch.
Oil on canvas. Ca. 1733.
John Smibert, American. 3919.20

156

Chest of Drawers with Panels of Oriental Lacquer. Ebony veneer, Japanese lacquer panels, gilt-bronze mounts. René Dubois, French, Paris, 1737-1799. 44.113*

Roman Ruins, Villa Pamfili. Dated 1774. Pen and brown ink; blue, gray, and red-brown water color. Hubert Robert, French. 51.485

Armchair (one of a pair). Carved and gilded wood. Jacques-Jean-Baptiste Tilliard (called Jean Baptiste II Tilliard), French, Paris, active 1752-1797. 27.424

Young Girl. Terra cotta. Claude Michel (called Clodion), French, 1738-1814. 42.50*

Satyress and Child. Terra cotta. 1803.
Claude Michel (called Clodion),
French. 63.251

Fire Dog (one of a pair). Gilt bronze.
France, ca. 1785. 44.126

Candelabrum. Bronze and gilt bronze
with marble base. Claude Michel
(called Clodion), French, 1738-1814.
44.124

Textile Panel. Silk, *lampas* weave,
brocaded and embroidered. France,
Lyon (design by Jean Démosthène
Dugourc), ca. 1790. 35.237

Candelabrum. Bronze, gilt bronze,
and gray marble. Claude Michel
(called Clodion), French, 1738-1814.
42.59

Work Table. Wood marquetry with
gilt-bronze mounts, Sèvres porcelain
top. Martin Carlin, French, Paris,
active 1766-1785. 42.594

Small Writing Table. Wood marquetry with gilt-bronze mounts. Jean-François Leleu, French, Paris, 1729-1807. 44.115

Armchair (one of a pair). Carved and partially gilded wood. Nicholas-Denis Delaisement, French, Paris, active 1776-after 1792. 44.110

Table. Mahogany with gilt-bronze mounts and white marble top. Adam Weisweiler, French, Paris, ca. 1750-ca.1809. 22.73

Stool. Made for Marie Antoinette's game room at Compiègne, but used at Fontainebleau. Carved and gilded wood. 1786-1787. Jean-Baptiste-Claude Sené, French, Paris. 54.385

Chair (one of a set of four). Carved, painted, and gilded wood with Beauvais tapestry covers. George Jacob, French, Paris, 1739-1814. 42.75

Tureen and Platter. Silver. 1798-1809. Henri Auguste, French, Paris. 52.592

Armchair (one of a set of six chairs and a settee). Carved and painted wood, covered in Aubusson tapestry after a design by Huet. Henri Jacob, French, Paris, 1753-1824. 42.30

Six Miniatures Mounted in an Oval Box. Dated 1779-1780(?). Gouache miniatures mounted in gold and enamel. Painted by Pierre Marie Gault de Saint-Germain, French, Paris. 57.409*

Rectangular Box. Enamel on gold. France, Paris, 1768-1769(?). 57.410

Lady Louisa Manners, Later Countess of Dysart, as Juno. Oil on canvas. Sir Thomas Lawrence, English, 1769-1830. 61.220

The Daughters of Colonel Thomas Carteret Hardy. Oil on canvas. 1801. Sir Thomas Lawrence, English 42.642

Portrait of Mrs. John Greene. Dated 1769. Oil on canvas. John Singleton Copley, American. 202.15

Mrs. West and Her Son Raphael. Oil on canvas. Ca. 1770. Benjamin West, American. 27.393

Portrait of Nathaniel Hurd. Oil on canvas. Ca. 1765. John Singleton Copley, American. 350.15*

Portrait of George Washington. Oil on canvas. Ca. 1790. Joseph Wright, American. 2552.21

Portrait of Mrs. John Thomson Mason. Oil on canvas. Ca. 1803. Gilbert Stuart, American. 21.428

Captain Jean T. David. Dated 1813. Oil on canvas. Thomas Sully, American. 1416.16

Portrait of Samuel Williams. Oil on canvas. Ca. 1818. Washington Allston, American. 65.474*

Marble Mantel. England, late 18th century. 44.471

Chair. From a set of furniture made for the Derby family, Salem. Carved mahogany with ebony feet. Attributed to Samuel McIntire, American, Salem, Massachusetts, 1757-1811. 62.125

Pair of Spurs. Silver. Paul Revere, Jr., American, Boston, 1735-1818. 40.252, 40.25

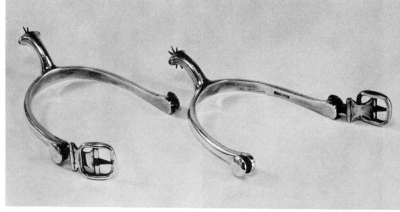

Plate. From a service made for Samuel Shaw. Porcelain. China, made for the American market, late 18th century. 61.178

Front Doorway. From the Isaac Gillet House, Painesville, Ohio. Carved and painted wood, glass and metal. Designed by Jonathan Goldsmith, American, Ohio, 1783-1847. 59.342

Centerpiece. Silver. 1808-1809. Paul Storr, English, London. 43.189*

Cupid and Psyche. Dated 1817. Oil on canvas. Jacques Louis David, French. 62.37*

Study of a Nude Woman, Seated Looking to the Right. Black and white chalk on blue paper. Pierre Paul Prud'hon, French, 1758-1823. 61.318*

Rosa Carolina Corymbosa. Water color on vellum. Pierre Joseph Redouté, French, 1759-1840. 59.15

La Citoyenne Crouzet. Oil on canvas. Ca. 1800. France, Circle of Jacques Louis David. 43.659

Portrait of Madame Raoul-Rochette.
Dated 1830. Pencil drawing. Jean
Auguste Dominique Ingres,
French. 27.437*

Antiochus and Stratonice. Oil on canvas. 1834. Jean Auguste Dominique
Ingres, French. 66.13

*Portrait of Comte Jean-Antoine
Chaptal.* Dated 1824. Oil on canvas.
Antoine Jean Gros, French. 64.54

166

Portrait of the Infante Don Luis de Borbón. Oil on canvas. 1783-84. Francisco de Goya y Lucientes, Spanish. 66.14*

Portrait of Don Juan Antonio Cuervo. Dated 1819. Oil on canvas. Francisco de Goya y Lucientes, Spanish. 43.90*

The Garroted Man. Etching, state I/II. Francisco de Goya y Lucientes, Spanish, 1746-1828. 63.470

Greek Pirates Attacking a Turkish Vessel. Dated 1827. Oil on canvas. Eugène Louis Gabriel Isabey, French. 16.1034

The Bulls of Bordeaux: The Celebrated American, Mariano Ceballos. Lithograph, state II/II. Francisco de Goya y Lucientes, Spanish, 1746-1828. 49.2

167

Mlle. Julie de la Boutraye. Oil on canvas. 1834. Eugène Delacroix, French. 62.3

Wild Horse. Dated 1828. Lithograph state I/II. Eugène Delacroix, French. 41.214

Armored Figure on Horseback. Pencil and sepia wash. Eugène Delacroix, French, 1798-1863. 33.418

Halt of the Greek Cavaliers. Dated 1858. Oil on canvas. Eugène Delacroix, French. 16.1032

Fighting Horses. Pencil and brown, blue, and black washes. Théodore Géricault, French, 1791-1824. 29.13*

The Roman Campagna. Oil on canvas. 1826-27. Jean Baptiste Camille Corot, French. 63.91*

Duchess of Ragusa. Dated 1818. On vellum. Jean-Baptiste Isabey, French. 42.1146

Woman Meditating. Oil on canvas. Jean Baptiste Camille Corot, French, 1796-1875. 49.189

Ville d'Avray, A Peasant Cutting Reeds in a Swamp.
Oil on canvas. Jean Baptiste Camille Corot,
French, 1796-1875. 44.80

Odalisque. Oil on canvas. Thomas Couture, French, 1815-1879. 39.63

Coast near Villerville. Dated 1855. Oil on canvas.
Charles François Daubigny, French. 51.323

Saint Etienne-du-Mont. Etching,
state I/VIII. 1852. Charles Meryon,
French. 55.528

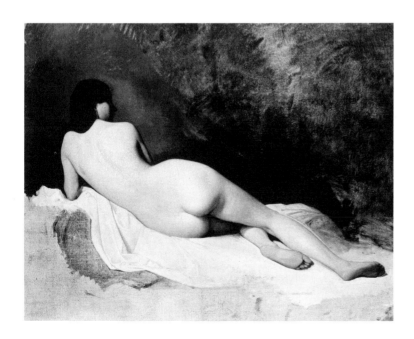

Connoisseurs. Charcoal, pencil, and water color. Honoré Daumier, French, 1808-1879. 27.208*

The Troubador. Oil on canvas. Honoré Daumier, French, 1808-1879. 58.23

Madame Boreau (La Dame au chapeau noir). Dated 1863. Oil on canvas. Gustave Courbet, French. 62.2

Grand Panorama of the Alps with the Dents du Midi. Oil on canvas. Ca. 1875. Gustave Courbet, French. 64.420

Stormy Sky at Trouville. Oil on canvas. Eugène Louis Boudin, French, 1825-1898. 66.208

At the Seashore. Dated 1864. Oil on wood. Eugène Louis
Boudin, French. 17.63

Summer. Dated 1891. Oil on canvas. Pierre Puvis de
Chavannes, French. 16.1056

Torso. Bronze, partially gilded.
Jules Dalou, French, 1838-1900. 18.571

Tannhäuser. Oil on canvas. Henri Fantin-Latour, French, 1836-1904. 16.1038

Mlle. Claire Campbell. Pastel. 1875. Edouard Manet, French. 56.718

Portrait of Berthe Morisot. Oil on canvas. Ca. 1869. Edouard Manet, French. 58.34

Boats. Oil on canvas. 1873. Edouard Manet, French. 40.534

Portrait of the Duchess of Montejasi-Cicerale. Oil on canvas. 1868. Hilaire-Germain Edgar Degas, French. 58.28*

Portrait of Diego Martelli. Charcoal and white chalk on brown paper. 1879 Hilaire-Germain Edgar Degas, French. 53.268*

Dancer Looking at the Sole of Her Right Foot. Bronze. Hilaire-Germain Edgar Degas, French, 1834-1917. 2028.47

Frieze of Dancers. Oil on canvas. 1883. Hilaire-Germain Edgar Degas, French. 46.83*

Mlle. Romaine Lacaux. Dated 1864. Oil on canvas. Pierre Auguste Renoir, French. 42.1065

Esterel Village. Monotype. Hilaire-Germain Edgar Degas, French, 1834-1917. 66.177

The Artist's Sister, Mme. Pontillon, Seated on the Grass. Oil on canvas. 1873. Berthe Morisot, French. 50.89

174

Spring Flowers. Dated 1864. Oil on canvas. Claude Oscar Monet, French. 53.155

Le Fond de l'Hermitage. Dated 1879. Oil on canvas. Camille Pissarro, French. 51.356

La Capeline Rouge—Mme. Monet. Oil on canvas. 1870-1875. Claude Oscar Monet, French. 58.39

The Cowherdess, Eragny. Charcoal. Camille Pissarro, French, 1830-1903. 2609.47

Ballet Girls. Pastel on paper, pasted on cardboard. Hilaire-Germain Edgar Degas, French, 1834-1917. 16.104

Race Horses. Pastel on cardboard. Ca. 1873-1875.
Hilaire-Germain Edgar Degas, French. 58.27

Low Tide at Pourville near Dieppe. Dated 1882.
Claude Oscar Monet, French. 47.196

The Age of Bronze. Bronze.
Auguste Rodin, French,
1840-1917. 18.328*

William E. Henley. Bronze. 1883.
Auguste Rodin, French. 40.581

Bust of Madame Rodin. Bronze.
Auguste Rodin, French,
1840-1917. 46.351

The Judgment of Paris. Bronze. 1914. Pierre Auguste Renoir (and Richard Guino), French. 41.591

Antibes. Oil on canvas. 1888. Claude Oscar Monet, French. 16.1044*

The Apple Seller. Oil on canvas. Ca. 1890. Pierre Auguste Renoir, French. 58.47

Three Bathers. Oil on canvas. 1897. Pierre Auguste Renoir, French. 39.269*

Young Woman Arranging Her Earrings. Oil on canvas. 1905. Pierre Auguste Renoir, French. 51.324

Siesta. Red chalk. Pierre Auguste Renoir, French, 1841-1919. 49.551

The Pigeon Tower at Montbriand. Oil on canvas. Ca. 1894-1896. Paul Cézanne, French. 36.19*

The Brook. Oil on canvas. 1898-1900. Paul Cézanne, French. 58.20

178

La Montagne Sainte-Victoire. Oil on canvas. 1894-1900.
Paul Cézanne, French. 58.21

Les Baigneurs (small plate). Lithograph printed in colors.
Paul Cézanne, French, 1839-1906. 63.598

Mademoiselle Ravoux. Oil on canvas.
1890. Vincent van Gogh, Dutch. 58.31

The Road Menders at Arles. Oil on canvas. 1889. Vincent van Gogh,
Dutch. 47.209

Poplars on a Hill. Oil on canvas. 1889. 1890. Vincent van Gogh, Dutch. 58.31

Monsieur Boileau at the Café. Gouache on cardboard. 1893. Henri de Toulouse-Lautrec, French. 394.25*

The Laundress. Brush and black ink, heightened with white on scratchboard. 1888. Henri de Toulouse-Lautrec, French. 52.113

May Belfort. Oil on cardboard. 1895. Henri de Toulouse-Lautrec, French. 58.54

The Jockey. Dated 1899. Lithograph. Henri de Toulouse-Lautrec, French. 26.125

Banks of the Seine at Suresnes. Oil on wood. 1883. Georges Seurat, French. 58.51

Rodin Working on 'The Gate of Hell.' Bronze. Emile Antoine Bourdelle, French, 1861-1929. 43.291

Café Concert. Conte crayon with touches of white. Georges Seurat, French, 1859-1891. 58.344

Portrait of Mademoiselle Violette Heymann. Dated 1910. Pastel on cardboard Odilon Redon, French.1976.26

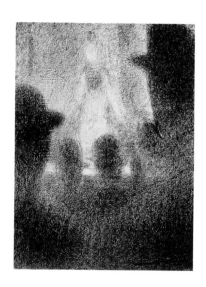

Vase of Flowers. Oil on canvas. Ca. 1905. Odilon Redon, French. 35.233

Yeux Clos. Lithograph. Odilon Redon, French, 1840-1916. 27.306

Orpheus. Pastel on cardboard. Odilon Redon, French, 1840-1916. 26.25*

L'Appel. Dated 1902. Oil on canvas. Paul Gauguin, French. 43.392*

Head of a Tahitian Woman. Pencil. Paul Gauguin, French, 1848-1903. 49.439*

The Café Wepler. Oil on canvas. Ca. 1905. Edouard Vuillard, French. 50.90

Under the Trees. Dated 1894.
Tempera on canvas. Edouard
Vuillard, French. 53.212

La Porte de Saint-Cloud. Dated 1904. Oil on canvas. Pierre Albert Marquet,
French. 61.263

General Duncan Campbell. Oil on canvas. Ca. 1806. Sir Henry Raeburn, English. 47.266

Burning of the Houses of Parliament, 1834. Oil on canvas. 1835. Joseph Mallord William Turner, English. 42.647*

Fluelen—Lake of Lucerne. Water color. Joseph Mallord William Turner, English, 1775-1851. 54.129

Tynemouth, Northumberland. Water color. Thomas Girtin, English, 1775-1802. 40.557

The Lonely Tower. Etching, state I/VI. 1879.
Samuel Palmer, English. 66.199

The Catskill Mountains. Dated 1833. Oil on canvas.
Thomas Cole, American. 1335.17

The Peaceable Kingdom. Oil on canvas. 1830.
Edward Hicks, American. 45.38

View of Florence from San Miniato. Oil on canvas. 1837.
Thomas Cole, American. 61.39

185

View near Newport. Oil on canvas. Ca. 1860.
John Frederick Kensett, American. 46.255

Twilight in the Wilderness. Dated 1860. Oil on canvas.
Frederic Edwin Church, American. 65.233*

Portrait of Gineo Scott. Dated 1859. Oil on canvas.
Eastman Johnson, American. 65.475

High Tide on the Marshes. Oil on canvas.
Martin Johnson Heade, American, 1819-1904. 490.15

Approaching Storm from Alban Hills. Dated 187(?). Oil on canvas. George Inness, American. 27.396

The Venetian Girl. Oil on canvas. Frank Duveneck, American, 1848-1919. 22.173

The Balcony. Etching, state I/XI. James McNeill Whistler, American, 1834-1903. 40.1088

Boy with the Anchor. Dated 1873. Water color on paper pasted on composition board. Winslow Homer, American. 54.128

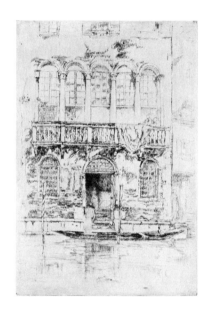

The Briarwood Pipe. Dated 1864. Oil on canvas. Winslow Homer, American. 44.524

Early Morning after a Storm at Sea. Oil on canvas. 1902. Winslow Homer, American. 24.195

Biglen Brothers Turning the Stake. Dated 1873. Oil on canvas. Thomas Eakins, American. 1984.27*

Study for Biglen Brothers Turning the Stake. Pencil with touches of light brown wash. Thomas Eakins, American, 1844-1916. 42.1066

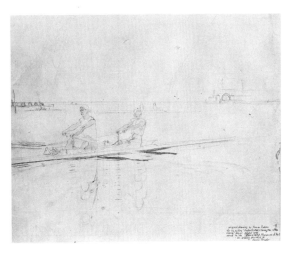

Rishi Calling up a Storm. Water color. John La Farge, American, 1835-1910. 39.267

The Race Track, or Death on a Pale Horse. Oil on canvas. Ca. 1910. Albert Pinkham Ryder, American. 28.8*

Portrait of Miss Dora Wheeler. Oil on canvas. 1883. William Merritt Chase, American. 21.1239

After the Bath. Pastel. Ca. 1901. Mary Cassatt, American. 20.379

The Visitor. Soft ground etching and aquatint, state II/V. Mary Cassatt, American, 1845-1926. 66.176

Fifth Avenue Nocturne. Oil on canvas. Ca. 1895. Childe Hassam, American. 52.538

Building a Dam, Shetucket. Oil on canvas. 1908. J. Alden Weir, American. 27.171

May Day, Central Park. Dated 1901. Water color. Maurice Prendergast, American. 26.17

The Drive, Central Park. Oil on canvas. Ca. 1905. William J. Glackens, American. 39.524

190

Self Portrait (George Bellows Drawing on a Stone in His Study). Lithograph. 1921. George Wesley Bellows, American. 35.279

Stag at Sharkey's. Oil on canvas. 1907. George Wesley Bellows, American. 1133.22

Holiday on the Hudson. Oil on canvas. Ca. 1912. George Benjamin Luks, American. 2291.33

Still Life. Oil on canvas. Preston Dickinson, American, 1891-1930. 1664.26

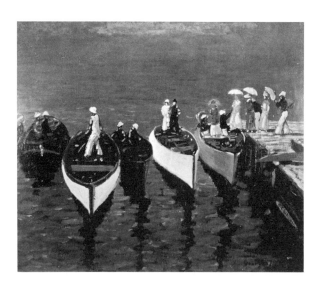

191

*Church Bells Ringing, Rainy Winter
Night.* Dated 1917. Water color.
Charles E. Burchfield, American. 49.544

The Sunflower Arch. Dated 1917.
Indelible pencil and crayon. Charles
E. Burchfield, American. 65.461

Woman's Work. Oil on canvas.
John Sloan, American, 1871-1951. 64.160

Fireworks. Dated 1926. Water color. George Overbury ("Pop") Hart,
American. 38.125

Hills, South Truro. Oil on canvas. 1930.
Edward Hopper, American. 2647.31

Markwippach III. Dated 1916. Charcoal.
Lyonel Feininger, American. 63.73

Houses in Old Paris. Woodcut. 1919.
Lyonel Feininger, American. 52.27

The Motor Boat. Oil on canvas. Dated 1931. Lyonel Feininger, American. 64.53

Landscape, New Mexico. Oil on canvas. Marsden Hartley, American. 1878-1943. 30.665

Rock and Sea, Small Point, Maine. Dated 1931. Oil on canvas. John Marin, American. 56.361

Storm-frightened Animals. Oil on canvas. 1933. Henry G. Keller, American. 34.56

194

Mountain Top. Water color. John Marin,
American, 1870-1953. 2731.30

Nude. Dated 1941. Brush drawing in
black and blue ink. John Flannagan,
American. 61.161

Horses in Snow. Water color. Ca. 1933.
William Sommer, American. 33.24

Deserted Farm. Oil on canvas. 1943. Max Weber, American. 210.46

Wounded Scoter, No. 2. Water color on rice paper mounted on cloth. 1944.
Morris Graves, American. 45.231

The St. Clair Fire. Dated 1944. Oil on masonite. Carl F. Gaertner,
American. 48.460

196

Melancholia: On the Beach. Woodcut colored by hand. 1896. Edvard Munch, Norwegian. 59.82

The Donkey Driver. Dated 1902. Pencil. Pablo Picasso, Spanish. 58.12

La Vie. Oil on canvas. 1903. Pablo Picasso, Spanish. 45.24*

Wrestlers in a Circus. Oil on canvas. 1906. Ernst Ludwig Kirchner, German. 66.49

Self Portrait with Hat. Oil on canvas. 1919. Karl Schmidt-Rottluff, German. 65.440

Torso. Brass. 1917. Constantine Brancusi, Romanian (French School). 3205.37

Mountain Landscape with Fir Trees. Pencil and brush and India ink. Ernst Ludwig Kirchner, German, 1880-1938. 63.86

Water Lilies. Oil on canvas. 1919-1926. Claude Monet, French. 60.81

Reclining Nude. Pen and ink on paper. 1938. Pablo Picasso, Spanish (French School). 63.151

Mother and Child. Bronze. 1929-30. Jacques Lipchitz, American. 55.166

The Wounded Soldier. Oil on canvas. 1930. José Clemente Orozco, Mexican. 54.864

Head of Christ. Oil on canvas. 1938. Georges Rouault, French. 50.399

Carnival at Nice. Oil on canvas. Henri Matisse, French, 1869-1954. 46.444

Potager à la Brunié. Oil on canvas. 1941. Jacques Villon, French. 64.95

Interior with Etruscan Vase. Oil on canvas. 1940. Henri Matisse, French. 52.153*

Constellation: Woman with Blond Armpit Combing Her Hair by the Light of the Stars. Oil and gouache on paper. 1940. Joan Miró, Spanish. 65.2*

Madonna and Child. Pen and ink wash. 1943. Henry Spencer Moore, British. 313.47

Mallarmé's Swan. Collage with gouache, crayon, and paper on cardboard. 1944. Robert Motherwell, American. 61.229*

Woman and Bird. Oil on canvas. 1944. Rufino Tamayo, Mexican. 50.583

Figure. Oil on cardboard. 1949. Willem de Kooning, American (born in Holland). 64.1

Lom-Lan. Oil on canvas. 1949-52. Victor Vasarely, Hungarian (French School). 65.427

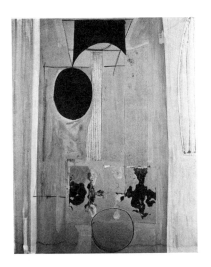

Mandrake. Steel brazed with copper. 1951. Theodore Roszak, American (born in Poland). 64.4

Video. Construction of mixed media. Joseph Cornell, American, b. 1903. 64.143

Woman with Child. Marble. 1958. Isamu Noguchi, American. 66.48

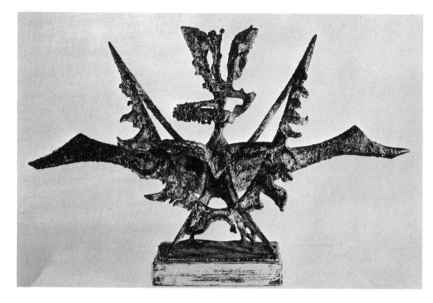

202

Sleeper I. Oil on canvas. 1958. Philip Guston, American (born in Canada). 61.21

Elegy to the Spanish Republic LV.
Oil on canvas. 1955-60.
Robert Motherwell, American. 63.583

Crest. Oil on canvas. 1959.
Jack Tworkov, American (born in
Poland). 62.33

*Smaragd Red and Germinating
Yellow.* Oil on canvas. 1959. Hans
Hofmann, American (born in
Germany). 60.57

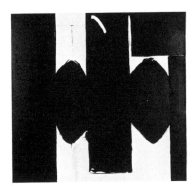

Red Maroons. Oil on canvas. 1962. Mark Rothko, American (born in Russia). 62.239*

Composition Concrete (Study for Mural). Oil on canvas. 1957-60. Stuart Davis, American. 64.2

Red Blue. Oil on canvas. 1962. Ellsworth Kelly, American. 64.142

Louis II. Oil on canvas. 1962. Richard Lindner, American (born in Germany). 65.450

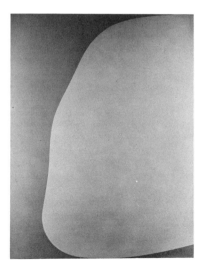

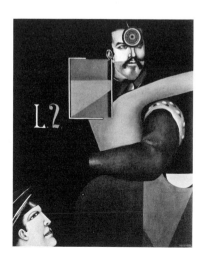

Notes

Notes

Notes

Islamic Art

Gold Ewer. Repoussé and engraved. Iran, Buyid Period, reign of Samsam al-Daula (985-998). 66.22

Hitching Post. Limestone. Iran, Seljuk Period, 13th century. 44.481

Tombstone. Marble. Iran, Seljuk Period, A.D. 1110. 50.9

End of Balustrade. Limestone. Iran, Hamadan, Mongol Period, 1304. 38.15

Lion Incense Burner. Bronze, cast and engraved. Iran, Seljuk Period, 12th century. 48.308

Bird-shaped Vessel. Bronze, cast and engraved, with turquoise eyes. Iran, Seljuk Period, 12th-13th century. 48.458

Ewer. Dated 1223. Brass, inlaid with silver. Made by Ahmad al-Dhaki, al-Naqsh, al-Mawsili, Mesopotamian (Iraq), Mosul. 56.11

Footed Bowl. Bronze, inlaid with silver. Iran, Seljuk Period, early 13th century. 44.485

Tray. Brass, inlaid with silver. Syria, mid-13th century. 45.386

Candlestick. Brass, inlaid with silver and engraved. Syria, 13th century. 51.539

Bottle. Enameled glass. Egypt or Syria, Mamluke Period, 14th century. 44.488

Box. Bronze, inlaid with gold and silver. Syria, 13th century. 44.482

Pottery Bowl. Luster ware. Egypt, Fustat, 11th century. 44.476

Pottery Bowl. Polychrome painted ware. Iran, Nishapur, 10th century. 56.225

Bowl. Enameled glass. Egypt or Syria, Mamluke Period, 14th century. 44.235

Pottery Bowl. Polychrome painted ware. Iran, Nishapur, 10th century. 59.249*

Pottery Bowl. Lakabi ware. Iran, 11th-12th century. 38.7*

Pottery Bowl. Champlevé ware. Iran, Garruz district, 11th-12th century. 38.8

Pottery Jug. Underglaze slip-painted ware. Iran, 12th century. 47.495

Pottery Plate. Luster ware. Iran, Gurgan, 12th-13th century. 51.289

Pottery Bottle. Luster ware. Iran, Rayy, 12th-13th century. 129.15

Pottery Bowl. Minai ware. Iran, Rayy, early 13th century. 39.214

Pottery Wall Tile. Luster ware. Iran, Kashan, 1266. 128.15

Pottery Beaker. Minai ware. Iran, Rayy, early 13th century. 898.17

Mihrab and Frieze. Faience mosaic tiles. Iran, Isfahan, 1st half 16th century. 62.23*

213

Textile Panel. Tapestry weave, wool and linen. Egypt, Abbasid Period, 1st half 9th century. 59.48*

Tiraz (detail). Silk tapestry on linen. Egypt, Fatimid Period, reign of al 'Aziz Bi'llah, 975-996. 50.354

Tiraz. Silk and gold tapestry on linen. Egypt, Fatimid Period, reign of Musta'li, 1094-1101. 65.313

Textile. Tapestry weave, silk and gold on linen. Egypt, Fatimid Period, late 11th century. 50.541

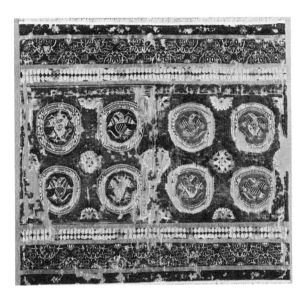

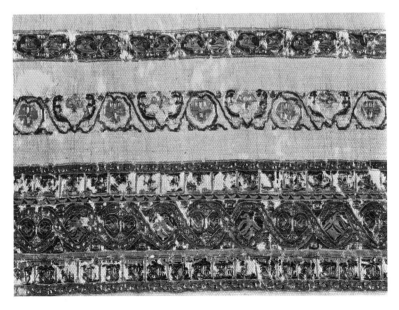

214

Textile. Tapestry weave, silk and
linen. Egypt, Fatimid Period, 1st half
12th century. 52.255

Textile. Diasper weave, silk. Egypt,
Ayyubid Period, 12th century. 37.23

Textile (detail). Embroidery, silk
and gold on *mulham.* Egypt or Sicily,
12th century. 50.533

Textile (detail). Diasper weave, silk
and gold. Egypt, Mamluke Period,
14th century. 39.40

Textile (detail). Printed on *mulham.*
Mesopotamia (Iraq), 10th century. 50.55

Tomb Cover. Compound twill, silk. Iran, Buyid Period, 10th century. 54.780

Fragment of a Tomb Cover. Compound twill, silk. Iran, Buyid Period, 998. 55.52*

Part of a Textile Panel. Diasper weave, silk. Iran, Buyid Period, 1003. 61.34

Textile Panel. Diasper weave, silk. Iran, Buyid Period, 10th-11th century. 62.264*

Textile (detail). Diasper weave, silk. Iran, Buyid Period, 10th-11th century. 50.84

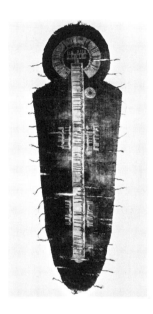

216

Textile (detail). Diasper weave, silk. Iran, Buyid Period, 10th-11th century. 53.434

Textile. Soumak weave, silk. Iran, Seljuk Period, 11th-12th century. 39.47

Textile. Velvet weave, silk and gold. Iran, Safavid Period, reign of Shah Tahmasp, 1524-1576. 48.205

Textile. Diasper weave, silk. Iran, Herat, Safavid Period, early 16th century. 24.743

Textile. Velvet weave, silk. Iran, Safavid Period, 2nd half 16th century. 44.499, 44.500

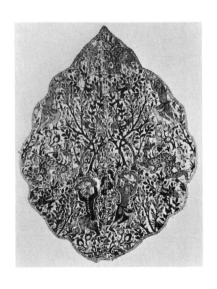

Fragment of a Carpet (detail). Senna knot, wool and cotton. Iran, Safavid Period, 16th century. 53.128

Textile (detail). Velvet weave, silk and gold. Iran, Safavid Period, 16th century. 44.239

Carpet (detail). Senna knot, wool and cotton. Iran, Herat, Safavid Period, 16th century. 62.263

Carpet. Senna knot, silk and cotton. Iran, Isfahan, Safavid Period, ca. 1600. 26.533

Textile. Velvet weave, silk and gold. Iran, Safavid Period, 17th century. 32.42*

Textile (detail). Diasper weave, silk and gold. Iran, Safavid Period, 17th century. 53.17

Textile (detail). Compound twill, silk. Spain, 11th-12th century. 51.92

Textile. Diasper weave, silk and gold. Spain, Almeria, Hispano-Islamic, 12th century. 50.146*

Textile. Diasper weave, silk and gold. Spain, Almeria, Hispano-Islamic, 12th century. 52.15

Textile. Compound weave, silk and gold. Spain, Almeria, Hispano-Islamic, 13th century. 32.137

Textile. Compound weave, silk and gold. Spain, Almeria, Hispano-Islamic, 13th century. 42.1077

Textile. Tapestry weave, silk and gold. Spain, Hispano-Islamic, 13th century. 52.105

Textile (detail). Diasper weave, silk and gold. Spain, Hispano-Islamic or Mudejar, 13th century. 52.106

Textile (detail). Tapestry weave, silk and gold. Spain, Almeria, Hispano-Islamic, 13th century. 28.650

Textile. Compound weave, silk, linen, and gold. Spain, Burgos, Mudejar, 13th century. 50.4

Textile. Diasper weave, silk and gold. Spain, Granada, Hispano-Islamic, 14th century. 39.35

Textile. Diasper twill, silk. Spain, Granada, Hispano-Islamic, 14th century. 46.417

Textile (detail). Diasper weave, silk. Spain, Granada, Hispano-Islamic, 14th century. 40.609

Textile (detail). Diasper weave, silk. Spain, Granada, Mudejar, 15th century. 29.83

Carpet (detail). Single knot, wool. Spain, Alcarez(?), Mudejar, 2nd half 15th century. 52.511

Illustration from a Manuscript of the Automata by Al-Jazari: Device for Washing Hands. Miniature painting. Mesopotamia (Iraq), 1315. 45.383

Illustration from a Manuscript of the Shahnamah of Firdawsi: Nushirwan's Fifth Banquet for Buzurdjmir. Miniature painting. Iran, Tabriz, Mongol Period, 1330-1340. 59.330

Illustration from a Manuscript of the Shahnamah of Firdawsi: Bahram Gur Slays a Dragon. Miniature painting. Iran, Tabriz School(?), Mongol Period, ca. 1330-1340. 43.658*

Double-page Frontispiece from a Manuscript of the Shahnamah of Firdawsi: Courtly Scene. Miniature painting. Iran, Shiraz, Timurid Period, ca. 1444. 45.169, 56.10*

Garden Scene. Miniature painting (unfinished). Iran, Herat, Timurid Period, style of Bihzad, late 15th century. 44.490

A Picnic in the Mountains. Line drawing with color. Iran, Tabriz, Safavid Period, style of Muhammadi, ca. 1550. 44.91

Illustration from a Manuscript of the Shahnamah of Firdawsi: Rustam meets the Challenge of Ashkabus. Miniature painting. Iran, Timurid Period, 15th century. 60.199

Ruler Seated in a Garden. Drawing with wash. Iran, Safavid Period, 16th century. 39.508

223

Illustration from the Khamsa of Nizami: An Episode from the Story of Khusraw and Shirin. Miniature painting. Iran, Safavid Period, 16th century. 47.500

Camel with Attendant. Drawing with wash. Safavid Period, mid-16th century. Attributed to Sultan Muhammad, Iranian. 44.849

Illustration from the Khamsa of Nizami: Nushirwan and the Owls. Miniature painting. Iran, Safavid Period, 16th century. 44.487

Youth Sleeping under a Willow Tree. Miniature painting. Iran, Safavid Period, late 16th century. 44.494

Illustration from a Manuscript: Courtly Procession. Miniature painting. Iran, Safavid Period, ca. 1600. 62.24

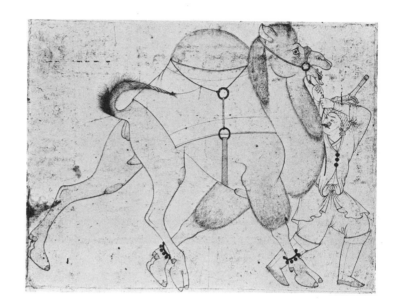

Dragon Combat. Drawing. Turkey, 15th century. 44.492

Youth with Toy. Miniature painting.
Iran, early 17th century. 47.497

Bookbinding. Leather, chased and perforated over gold. Iran, 15th century. 44.49

Notes

Notes

Far Eastern Art

Male Head with Turban. Red sandstone. India, Shunga Period, 185-72 B.C. 62.45*

Bacchanalian Scene. Schist. India, Gandhara, from Buner, 1st-2nd century. 30.329

Pendant with Deity Hariti. Gold and carnelian. India, Sirkap, Saka-Parthian Period, ca. 50 B.C.-A.D. 50. 53.14

Seated Buddha. Gray schist. India, Gandhara, 3rd century. 61.418*

Bodhisattva. Gray schist. India, Gandhara, 3rd century. 65.476

Torso of a Chauri Bearer. Red sandstone. India, Kushan Period, 2nd century. 65.472

Adoring Attendant. From a Buddhist shrine. Stucco. India, Hadda (Afghanistan), 5th century. 43.395

Standing Maitreya. Red sandstone. India, Kushan Period, 3rd century. 43.661

Lion. Red sandstone. India, Kushan Period, 1st-2nd century. 52.514

Seated Ascetics. Two terra-cotta plaques. Harwan, Kashmir, 2nd century. 59.131, 59.132

Scene of Worship (Fragment of Casing Slab). Marble. India, Nagarjunakonda, Satavahana Dynasty, late 2nd-early 3rd century. 43.72

Head of a Buddha. Red sandstone. India, Gupta Period, 4th-5th century. 63.504*

Seated Buddha. Red sandstone. India, Proto-Gupta Period, 3rd century. 41.94

Standing Buddha. Cream sandstone. India, Gupta Period, from Sarnath, 5th century. 43.278

Head of Vishnu. Red sandstone. India, Gupta Period, 5th century. 42.498

Standing Vishnu. Stone. India, Mathura Region. Gupta Period, ca. 600. 63.580

Ganga, Goddess of the Ganges. Stone India, Mathura, early 7th century. 66.119

Surya, the Sun God. Brass. Kashmir, early 8th century. 65.557

Standing Buddha. Brass. North India or Kashmir, early 8th century. 66.30*

Buddha Calling on the Earth to Witness. Black chlorite. India, Bengal, Pala Dynasty, 9th century. 35.146*

Chakrapurusa: Angel of the Discus. Black chlorite. India, Apshad, Pala Dynasty, ca. 670. 45.367

Manjushri, Lord of Wisdom. Image of gilded copper; pedestal and mandorla of brass. India, Bengal, Pala Dynasty, 11th-12th century. 60.285

Shiva and Parvati: Umamaheshvara. Bronze. India, Pala Dynasty, Reign of Devapala, 815-854. 64.50*

233

Vishnu Attended by Chakrapurusa and Shankhapurusa. Bronze with silver inlay. North India, Pala Dynasty, ca. 12th century. 64.453

Vasudhara: Goddess of Abundance. Copper gilt with inlaid gems. Nepal, 14th-15th century. 47.493

Gandavyuha (detail). Illuminated manuscript, ink and color on palm leaf. India, Bengal, Pala Dynasty, 11th-12th century. 55.49

Astasahasrika Prajnaparamita: Book of Transcendental Wisdom (detail). Illustrated manuscript, color on wood and palm leaf. India, Bengal(?), 1110. 38.301

234

Manjushri, Bodhisattva of Wisdom.
Gilt copper. Nepal, 16th century. 56.8

Vasya-Vajravarahi (Dancing Deity).
Stucco. Nepal, 16th-17th century.
64.103

Bodhisattva Manjushri Jananasathva.
Gilt bronze. Nepal, late 16th century.
64.370*

Dancing Ganesha. Red sandstone.
India, Khajuraho Region, 1000. 61.93

Mithuna (Lovers). Stone. India, from
Rajputana, from Harsagiri, 973. 62.165

235

Vaishnava Trinity: Shri Devi, Vishnu, Bhu Devi. Granite. India, probably from Region of Pudokkatai, early Chola Period, 1st half 10th century. 63.104-63.106*

Shiva: Gajasura-samharamurti. Granite. South India, Early Chola Period, 11th century. 62.164

Shiva and Parvati: Uma-sahita Murti. Copper. South India, early Chola Period, early 10th century. 61.94*

Shiva and Parvati: Alingana-Chandrasekhara-Murti. Copper. South India, Chola Period, 11th-12th century. 54.7

Shiva Nataraja. Copper. South India, Chola Period, 11th century. 30.331*

A Guardian of Shiva. Stone. India, Hoysala Dynasty, Mysore, 13th century. 64.369*

Manuscript of the Tuti-Nama by Ziya al-din Nakhshabi: fol. 110 v, A Poet-Musician. Color and gold on paper (manuscript almost complete). India, Mughal, early reign of Akbar, ca. 1560. 62.279*

King Parikshit and Rishis. Color on paper. South Rajathan or Central India, Mandu, ca. 1550. 60.53

Siege of Arbela. Color on paper with gold. Late 16th century. Designed by Basawan, painted by Sur Gujarati, Indian, Mughal. 47.502

Page from Ta'rikh-i-alfi (History of a Thousand Years). Color on paper. India, Mughal School, late 16th century. 32.36

Imperial Rooster. Color on paper. Early 17th century. Signed: Dilaram Padarat Kashmiri. Indian, Mughal. 44.501

Page from a Razm Nama. Dated 1616. Color on paper. India, Mughal. 60.44

Hunting Scene. Color on paper. India, Mughal, early 17th century. 39.66

238

Madhu Madhavi Ragini. Color on paper. India, Malwa, Rajput, ca. 1630. 25.1336

Krishna: from a Rasikapriya. Color on paper. India, Malwa, Rajput, 1634. 38.303

Khandita Nayaka: The Errant Lover. Color on paper. North India, Rajasthan, Mewar-Udaipur School, ca. 1630. 60.52

Sadh-malara Ragini. Color on paper. Central India, Rajasthani, Malwa style, ca. 1650. 60.116

Panchama Ragini. Color on paper. India, Mewar, Rajput, ca. 1680. 31.451

Gajahamurti: Shiva and Parvati after the Death of the Elephant Demon. Color on paper. India, Punjab, Basohli School, ca. 1700. 52.587

Durga Slaying Mahisha. Color on paper. India, Punjab, Basohli School, ca. 1700. 60.51

Sita in the Garden of Lanka with Ravana and His Demons: The Siege of Lanka sequence, from *The Ramayana.* Gold and color on paper. India, Rajputana, Punjab Hills, Guler, ca. 1720. 66.143*

Rajah Smoking with Son and a Courtier. Color on paper. North India, Punjab, Jammu School, ca. 1730. 60.47

Krishna Awaiting Radha. Color on paper. India, Rajput, Guler, ca. 1760. 36.685

Toilette of Radha. Colors on paper, gold. India, Rajput, Kangra School, ca. 1800. 53.245

Palace Ladies Hunting from a *Pavilion.* Color and gold on paper. India, Rajasthan, Kotah School, ca. 1760-1770. 55.48*

Pendant in Shape of Pipal Leaf. Gold with enamel in champlevé technique. India, Rajputana, 16th-17th centry. 46.257

Durga Slaying Mahisha. Color on paper. India, Pahari, Kangra School, late 18th century. 55.667

Carpet (detail). Senna knot, silk. India, Mogul Period, early 17th centur 36.17

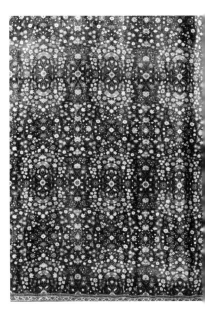

Textile (detail). Diasper weave, silk. India, Rajput, Jaipur, 17th century. 53.474

Buddha with Hands in Gesture of Teaching, Vitarka Mudra. Bronze. Siam, Thailand, Mon Dvaravati Period, 7th century. 58.334

Head of Buddha. Sandstone, bluish gray. Cambodia, Pre-Angkorean, style of Tra Vinh, late 6th-early 7th century. 32.43

Vishnu. Gray sandstone. Cambodia, Pre-Angkorean, style of Prasat Andet, 2nd half 7th century. 42.562*

Head of Shiva. Tan sandstone. Cambodia, style of Koh Ker, reign of Jayavarman IV, 928-941. 40.53*

Shiva. Gray sandstone. Cambodia, style of Baphuon, 1st half 11th century. 41.25

Buddha Enthroned. Bronze altarpiece. Cambodia, Period of Angkor Wat, ca. 1112-1153. 42.149

Finial. Bronze. Cambodia, ca. 1200. 64.93

Dancing Apsaras: Heavenly Beings. Section of a lintel from the Bayon of Angkor Thom. Sandstone. Cambodia, reign of Jayavarman VII, ca. 1181-1218. 38.433

243

*Buddha Sheltered by Mucalinda,
the Serpent King.* Bronze. Cambodia,
Period of Angkor Wat, early
12th century. 63.263*

Shiva. Sandstone. Champa, from
Dong-duong, Indrapura, 9th century.
35.147

Lokeshvara. Sandstone. Cambodia,
reign of Jayavarman VII, Second
Angkorean Period, 1002-1201. 55.47

Padmapani. Copper. Java, Sailendra
Period, 8th-9th century. 54.125

Princess. From the Terrace of the
Leper King Angkor Thom. Sandstone.
Cambodia, reign of Jayavarman VII,
ca. 1181-1218. 38.304

Head of Buddha. Black lava stone.
Java, from Borobudur, early
9th century. 42.1087

Vase: Pan-shan Type. Painted pottery. China, Kansu Province, Neolithic Period, 2500-1500 B.C. 30.332

Ting: Tripod. Bronze. China, Shang Dynasty, 11th century B.C. 62.281

Axe. Bronze. China, Shang Dynasty, 1523-1028 B.C. 37.27

Fang-yu: Square Wine Container. Bronze. China, late Shang Dynasty, 12th-11th century B.C. 63.103*

Ku: Beaker. Bronze. China, Shang Dynasty, 13th-12th century B.C. 60.43

Mask. Marble. China, Shang Dynasty, ca. 1200 B.C. 52.585

Elephant-feline Head. Jade, partly calcified. China, Shang Dynasty, ca. 1200 B.C. 52.573

Tsun: Owl. Bronze. China, Shang or early Western Chou Period, 1027-771 B.C. 51.119

Tsun: Ceremonial Vessel. Bronze. China, early Chou Period, 1027-ca. 900 B.C. 51.151

Li-ting: Hollow-legged Tripod. Bronze. China, reportedly from Hsi-an, Early Chou Period, 1027-ca. 900 B.C. 61.203*

Hu: Covered Vessel. Bronze. China, middle Chou Period, ca. 900-ca. 600 B.C. 44.61

Staff Finial. Bronze. China, from Chin-Ts'un, Period of Warring States, ca. 481-221 B.C. 30.730*

Po: Bell. Bronze. China, late Chou Period, early 5th century B.C. 62.44

Cranes and Serpents. Lacquered wood. China, from Ch'ang-sha, Period of Warring States, 481-221 B.C. 38.9*

Interlace Plaque. Honey-colored jade. China, from Ch'ang-sha, late Chou Period, ca. 600-221 B.C. 52.584

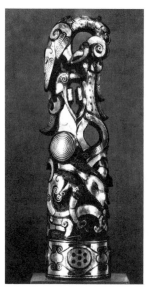

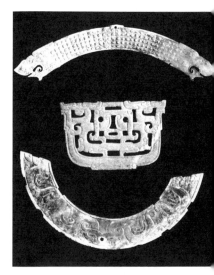

The Kill. Carved and painted shell.
China, late Chou or early Han
Dynasty, 4th-3rd century B.C. 57.139

Relief. Stone. China, from Szechwan,
Han Dynasty, 206 B.C.-A.D. 220. 62.280

Vase and Cover. Green lead glaze
over red clay body. China, Han
Dynasty, 206 B.C.-A.D. 220. 24.196

Hill Jar. Lead-glazed pottery. China,
Han Dynasty, 206 B.C.-A.D. 220. 48.214

Vase. Porcelain with ash glaze.
China, late Chou or early Han
Dynasty, 4th-3rd century B.C. 54.370

Top of a Hun-p'ing: Urn of the Soul.
Yueh ware. China, from Shao-hsing,
Six Dynasties, Wu, 222-280, or
Western Chin, 265-316. 60.76

Pole Top: Wild Ass. Cast bronze,
hollow. China, Ordos Region, Han
Dynasty, 206 B.C.-A.D. 220. 62.46

*Two Reliefs from a Funerary Stone
Model.* Terra cotta. China, Han
Dynasty, 206 B.C.-A.D. 220
25.134, 25.135

Tomb Tile (detail). Terra cotta. China, late Han Dynasty, 2nd-3rd century. 15.7

P'u-shou: Monster-head Door-ring Holder. Gilt bronze. China, Six Dynasties, 220-589. 30.731

Maitreya and Attendants. Dated 500. Sandstone. China, Northern Wei Dynasty. 59.130

Adoring Monk. Gilt bronze. China, Northern Wei Period, ca. 520-525. 62.213

Mortuary Horse. Painted pottery. China, Northern Wei Period, 386-535. 29.985

Head of Bodhisattva Kuan-yin. Stone. China, from Lung-men, Northern Wei Period, ca. 510-520. 15.77

Stele: Sakyamuni Trinity. Dated 537.
Limestone. China, Eastern Wei
Period. 420.14

Squatting Caryatid Monster.
Limestone. China, from Northern
Hsiang-t'ang-shan, Northern Ch'i
Period, ca. 570. 57.360

Stele: Maitreya, as the Future Buddha.
Marble. China, Northern Ch'i
Period, 550-577. 17.320

Bodhisattva Kuan-yin. Sandstone.
with polychrome. China, Sui Dynasty,
581-618. 62.162

Guardian Lion. White marble. China,
Sui or early T'ang Dynasty, ca. 600.
65.473

Candlestick. White porcellaneous ware, greenish-white glaze. China, Sui Dynasty, 581-618, or early T'ang Dynasty, 618-907. 30.322

Jar. Lead-glazed pottery. China, T'ang Dynasty, 618-907. 40.44

Horse. Lead-glazed pottery. China, T'ang Dynasty, 618-907. 55.295

A Harpist. Lead-glazed terra cotta. China, T'ang Dynasty, 618-907. 31.450

Bull. Painted pottery. China, T'ang Dynasty, 618-907. 29.987

Jar. Cream-glaze pottery. China,
T'ang Dynasty, 618-907. 30.323

Jar. Porcelain, Hsing ware. China,
T'ang Dynasty, 618-907. 57.29

Ewer in the Form of a Court Lady.
Porcellaneous ware. North China,
Liao Kingdom, 937-1125. 53.248

Stem Cup. Gilded silver. China,
T'ang Dynasty, 618-907. 51.396

Amitabha Buddha. Limestone. China,
early T'ang Dynasty, 618-907. 64.152

Kuan-yin. Marble. China, early T'ang Dynasty, 618-907. 29.981

Eleven-headed Kuan-yin. Gray sandstone. China, T'ang Dynasty, 1st quarter 8th century. 59.129*

Dancing Apsaras. Dry lacquer. China, late T'ang or early Five Dynasties, 9th-10th century. 53.356

Textile. Silk, patterned weave. China, 8th century. 54.109

Amitabha Buddha, Seated. Gilt bronze. China, Liao Kingdom, 10th century. 42.1082

Taoist Figure. Wood and ivory. China, Southern Sung Dynasty, 1127-1279. 64.368

Potala Kuan-yin. Sandalwood. China, Five Dynasties, 10th century. 65.556

Bodhisattva. Cypress. China, Southern Sung Dynasty, 13th century. 63.581

Vase. Stoneware, Tz'u-chou ware. China, Sung Dynasty or earlier, 960-1279. 42.656

255

Jar. Stoneware, Tz'u-chou ware. China, Sung Dynasty, 960-1279. 48.225

Meip'ing: Gallipot Vase. Stoneware, Tz'u-chou ware. China, Northern Sung Dynasty, 960-1127. 40.52

Vase. Stoneware, Tz'u-chou ware, "Chiao-ts'o" type. China, Northern Sung Dynasty, 960-1127. 48.226*

Lion. Porcelain, Yueh ware. China, Northern Sung Dynasty, 960-1127. 66.26

Teapot. Stoneware, Tz'u-chou ware. China, Sung Dynasty, 960-1279. 48.219

Phoenix-headed Vase. Porcelain, Ch'ing-pai ware. China, Sung Dynasty, 960-1279. 65.468*

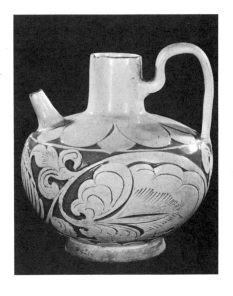

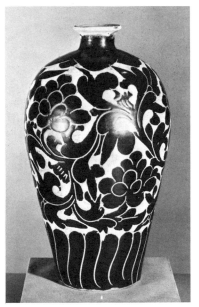

Covered Box. White porcelain, Ting ware. China, Northern Sung Dynasty, 960-1127. 57.32

Circular Washer. Porcelain, Ju ware. China, Northern Sung Dynasty, 960-1127. 57.40

Covered Box with Carved Floral Design. Porcelain, northern celadon ware. China, Northern Sung Dynasty, 960-1127. 62.41

Plate. Porcellaneous stoneware, Chun ware. China, Sung Dynasty, 960-1279. 42.665

Teapot. Porcelain, Tung ware. China, Northern Sung Dynasty, 960-1127. 48.220*

Flower Pot Stand. Porcellaneous stoneware, Chun ware. China, Sung Dynasty, 960-1279. 57.33

Ting: Tripod. Celadon, Lung-ch'uan ware. China, Southern Sung Dynasty, 1127-1279. 54.790

Althea Bowl. Kuan ware. China, Southern Sung Dynasty, 1127-1279. 57.66

Ch'a-tou: Vase in Grain Measure Shape. Lung-ch'uan ware. China, Southern Sung Dynasty, 1127-1279. 57.73

Lu: Incense Burner. Porcellaneous stoneware, Kuan ware. China, Southern Sung Dynasty, 1127-1279. 57.63*

Washer Basin. From Phoenix Hill Kiln, Hangchou. Kuan ware. China, Southern Sung Dynasty, 1127-1279. 57.48

Barbarian Royalty Worshiping Buddha. Handscroll, ink and color on silk. Traditionally attributed to Chao Kuang-fu, Chinese, active 960-975, Northern Sung Dynasty. 57.358

Ch'i-shan-wu-chin: Streams and Mountains without End. Handscroll, ink on silk. China, Northern Sung Dynasty, early 12th century. 53.126*

Buddhist Monastery by Stream and Mountains. Hanging scroll, ink on silk. Attributed to Chu Jan, Chinese, active ca. 960-980, Northern Sung Dynasty. 59.348*

Cloudy Mountains. Dated 1130. Handscroll, ink and sligh color on silk. Mi Yu-jen, Chinese, Sung Dynasty. 33.220*

Cottages in a Misty Grove in Autumn. Dated 1117. Album leaf, ink and color on silk. Li An-chung, Chinese, Northern Sung Dynasty. 63.588

The Knick-Knack Peddler. Dated 1212. Album leaf, ink and slight color on silk. Li Sung, Chinese, Southern Sung Dynasty. 63.582*

Birds in a Grove in a Mountainous Landscape in Winter. Hanging scroll, ink and slight color on silk. Kao Tao, Chinese, Sung Dynasty, 12th century. 66.115

Scholar Reclining and Watching Rising Clouds. Dated 1256. Fan painting, ink and slight color on silk. Ma Lin, Chinese, Southern Sung Dynasty. 61.421

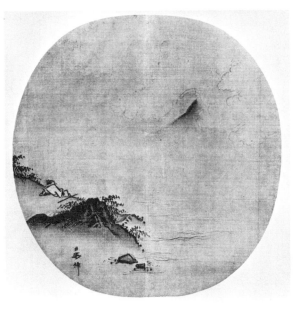

Tiger. Hanging scroll, ink on silk. Attributed to Mu-ch'i, Chinese, active 2nd half 13th century, Southern Sung Dynasty. 58.428

P'an: Plate with Biscuit-reserved Dragon. Porcelain. China, Yuan Dynasty, 14th century. 61.92

The Bodhisattva P'u-hsien: Samantabhadra. Hanging scroll, color and ink on silk. China, Southern Sung Dynasty, 1127-1279. 62.161

K'uan: Jar. Porcelain with blue underglaze decorations. China, Yuan Dynasty, 14th century. 62.154

Jar. Tz'u-chou ware. China, Yuan Dynasty, 1280-1368. 48.215

Bowl with Taoist Design. White jade. China, Yuan Dynasty, 1280-1368. 52.510

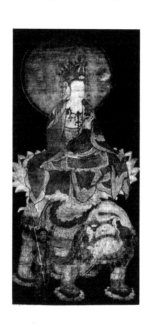

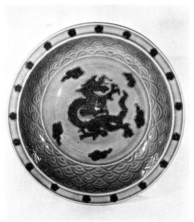

261

The Lantern Night Excursion of Chung K'uei (detail). Handscroll, ink on silk. Yen Hui, Chinese, Yuan Dynasty, 1280-1368. 61.206

Chin-ko-t'u: The Nine Songs. Handscroll, ink on paper. Chang Wu, Chinese, active 1335-1365, Yuan Dynasty. 59.138

Bodhidharma Crossing the Yangtze on a Reed. Hanging scroll, ink on paper. China, Yuan Dynasty, 1280-1368. 64.44

Shakyamuni. Gilt bronze. China, Yuan Dynasty. 66.116

262

Three Horses and Four Grooms (detail). Handscroll, ink and color on silk. Jen Jen-fa, Chinese, 1254-1327, early Yuan Dynasty. 60.181

Poetic Feeling in a Thatched Pavilion. Dated 1347. Handscroll, ink on paper. Wu Chen, Chinese, Yuan Dynasty. 63.259

Bamboos, Rocks, and Lonely Orchids. Handscroll, ink on paper. Chao Meng-fu, Chinese, 1254-1322, Yuan Dynasty. 63.515*

The Scholar's Leisure. Dated 1360. Handscroll, ink on paper. Yao T'ing-mei, Chinese, Yuan Dynasty. 54.263

Chrysanthemums and Cabbage. Dated 1490. Handscroll, ink and slight color on paper. T'ao Cheng, Chinese, Ming Dynasty. 60.40

The Poet Lin P'u Wandering in the Moonlight. Hanging scroll, ink and slight color on paper. Tu Chin, Chinese, active ca. 1465-1487, Ming Dynasty. 54.582

A Distant View of Tiger Hill, from *Twelve Views of Tiger Hill, Suchou.* Leaf from album, ink on paper. Shen Chou, Chinese, 1427-1509, Ming Dynasty. 64.371*

Old Pine Tree. Handscroll, ink on paper. Wen Cheng-ming, Chinese, 1470-1559, Ming Dynasty. 64.43

Beggars and Street Characters (detail). Dated 1516. Handscroll, ink and color on paper. Chou Chen, Chinese, Ming Dynasty. 64.94

Chao Meng-fu Writing the Heart Sutra in Exchange for Tea (detail). Dated 1543. Color on paper. Ch'iu Ying, Chinese, Ming Dynasty.

Autumn Mountains. Tribute from the Korean king to the throne of Ming Emperor Sheng-tsung. Handscroll, ink on paper. Tung Ch'i-ch'ang, Chinese, 1555-1636, Ming Dynasty. 59.46

Greeting the Spring. Dated 1600. Handscroll, color and ink on paper. Wu Pin, Chinese, Ming Dynasty. 59.45

Lady Hsuan-wen-chun Giving Instructions on the Classics. Dated 1638. Hanging scroll, color on silk. Ch'en Hung-shou, Chinese, Ming Dynasty. 61.89

Chueh: Tripod. Imperial white porcelain. China, Ming Dynasty, reign of Yung Lo, 1403-1424. 57.59

Pa-pei: Stem Cup. Porcelain, blue underglaze, red enamel overglaze. China, Ming Dynasty, mark and reign of Hsuan Te, 1426-1435. 57.60

Dish. White porcelain, underglaze in Mohammedan blue. China, Ming Dynasty, reign of Hsuan Te, 1426-1435. 53.127*

Wine Cup. Porcelain with blue underglaze and overglaze in red and green enamels, Tou Tsai ware. China, Ming Dynasty, mark and reign of Ch'eng Hua, 1465-1487. 57.61*

Bowl with Land of Taoist Immortals Scene. Porcelain with blue underglaze decorations. China, Ming Dynasty, mark and reign of Hsuan Te, 1426-1435. 62.2◆

Dice Bowl with Decorations of the Three Friends. White porcelain, blue underglaze. China, Ming Dynasty, mark and reign of Hsuan Te, 1426-1435. 53.631

Covered Jar. Porcelain, blue underglaze, overglaze in red, green, and yellow enamels. China, Ming Dynasty, mark and reign of Wan Li, 1573-1619. 57.62

Vase. Porcelain, "yellow family." China, Ming Dynasty, 1368-1644. 42.718

Kuan-yin of the South Sea. White porcelain, Te-hua ware. China, Ming Dynasty, 1368-1644. 50.579

Meip'ing Vase. Porcelain. China, Ming Dynasty, 1368-1644. 42.716

Reclining Water Buffalo. Jade. China, early Ming Dynasty, 1368-1644. 60.282

268

Hoop-backed Armchair: "Lohan Type." Burmese or East Indian rosewood. China, Ming Dynasty, 1368-1644. 55.40

Fragment of a Panel. Tapestry weave (k'o-ssu), silk and gold. China, Ming Dynasty, 1368-1644. 16.1334

One Leaf from Reminiscences of Ch'in-Huai River. Eight-leaf album, ink and color on paper. Shih-t'ao (Tao-chi), Chinese, ca. 1630-after 1707, Ch'ing Dynasty. 66.31*

Pure Tones of the Hills and Waters. Dated 1664. Handscroll, ink and color on paper. Hsiao Yun-ts'ung, Chinese, Ch'ing Dynasty. 54.262

Landscape Album, in Various Styles. Dated 1684. Ink and color on paper. Ch'a Shih-piao, Chinese, Ch'ing Dynasty. 55.37

269

Bamboo Grove and Distant Mountains.
Dated 1694. Hanging scroll, ink on
paper. Wang Hui, Chinese, Ch'ing
Dynasty. 53.629

Landscape after Ni Tsan. Dated 1707.
Hanging scroll, ink and color on paper.
Wang Yuan-ch'i, Chinese, Ch'ing
Dynasty. 54.583

Pine Wind from Myriad Valleys.
Hanging scroll, ink and color on
paper. Wu Li, Chinese, 1632-1718,
Ch'ing Dynasty. 54.584

Conversation in Autumn. Dated 1732.
Hanging scroll, ink and color on paper.
Hua Yen, Chinese, Ch'ing Dynasty.
54.263*

*Drunken Chung K'uei Supported by
Ghosts.* Hanging scroll, ink and color
on paper. Lo P'ing, Chinese, 1733-1799,
Ch'ing Dynasty. 59.185

Bottle-shaped Vase. Lang ware, "ox-blood" glaze. China, Ch'ing Dynasty, reign of K'ang Hsi, 1662-1722. 44.201

Vase. Porcelain, "peach-bloom" glaze. China, Ch'ing Dynasty, mark and reign of K'ang Hsi, 1662-1722. 42.669

Baluster Vase. Porcelain, "black family." China, Ch'ing Dynasty, Reign of K'ang Hsi, 1662-1722. 42.696

Vase. Porcelain, "soft paste," blue underglaze. China, Ch'ing Dynasty, mark and reign of Yung Cheng, 1723-1735. 42.728

271

Vase. Porcelain, "green family." China, Ch'ing Dynasty, reign of K'ang Hsi, 1662-1722. 42.685

Vase, Ku-yueh-hsuan Type. Porcelain with decoration in colored *fa-lang* enamels. China, Ch'ing Dynasty, enameled mark and reign of Ch'ien Lung, 1736-1795. 63.514

Vase, Ku-yueh-hsuan Type. Porcelain, "rouge de fer" handles, black and colored enamels. China, Ch'ing Dynasty, reign of Ch'ien Lung, 1736-1795. 42.712

Koro with T'ao-t'ieh Masks. Green jade. China, Ch'ing Dynasty, Ch'ien Lung Period, 1736-1795. 42.620

272

Vase. Porcelain. Korea, Koryu Period, 12th or 13th century. 44.164

Bottle Vase with Fish Design. Punch'ong stoneware. Korea, Yi Dynasty, 15th century. 62.153

Haniwa Figure. Terra cotta. Japan, Kofun Period, 200-552. 62.39

Dotaku: Bell. Bronze. Japan, late Yayoi Period, A.D. 100-300. 16.1102

Urn. Terra cotta. Japan, Middle Jomon Period, ca. 1000 B.C. 60.196

Heavenly Musician. From Horyu-ji, Nara. Camphor wood with polychrome. Japan, Hakuho Period, 645-710. 54.792

Hanka-shiyui-zo: Maitreya in Meditation. Bronze. Japan, Suiko Period, 7th century. 50.86

Kwannon: Avalokiteshvara. Gilt bronze. Japan, Hakuho Period, 645-710. 50.392

Woman from an Audience Scene. Probably from Horyu-ji, Nara. Gray unbaked clay. Japan, Hakuho Period, 645-710. 50.393

Suikoju: Gigaku Mask. Paulownia wood, lacquered and painted. Japan, Tempyo Period, 710-794. 49.158

Hand of Buddha. Wood. Japan, late Nara or early Jogan Period, late 8th-early 9th century. 56.126

Bosatsu, Gyodo Mask. Lacquered wood with paint. Japan, Fujiwara Period, 12th century. 50.581

Nikko, the Sun Bodhisattva. Carved from one block of Japanese yew. Japan Konin Period, ca. 800. 61.48*

Godai-Kokuzo: Five Bodhisattvas of the Mandala of the Void. Gilded wood. Japan, Fujiwara Period, 897-1185. 64.45-64.49

Amida's Paradise. Lacquer, fragment mounted as a box cover. Japan, ca. 1200. 61.91

275

Box with Chrysanthemum Design. Lacquer. Japan, Kamakura Period, 1185-1333. 63.513

Kwannon. Lacquered wood with kirikane decoration. Japan, Kamakura Period, 13th century. 52.90

Shinto Deity: Izu-san Gongen. Wood. Japan, Kamakura Period, 12th-13th century. 54.373

Amida, Buddha of the Western Paradise. Dated 1269. Wood with cut gold leaf, polychrome. Koshun and assistants, Japanese, Kamakura Period. 60.197

Kara-shishi ("China Lion"). Wood. Japan, Kamakura Period. 24.352

Gohimitsu Bosatsu: The "Secret Five" Bodhisattva. Hanging scroll, color, gold, and silver on three joined pieces of silk. Japan, Kamakura Period, late 12th century. 61.423*

Kasuga Mandala. Hanging scroll, ink on silk. Japan, Muromachi Period, 1392-1573. 17.93

Nika Byakudo: The White Path to the Western Paradise across Two Rivers. Hanging scroll, ink and color on silk. Japan, Kamakura Period, 13th-14th century. 55.44

One of the "Ten Fast Bulls." Hanging scroll, ink and slight color on paper, from a handscroll. Japan, Kamakura Period, mid-13th century. 52.286

Kumano Mandala: The Three Sacred Shrines. Hanging scroll, color on silk. Japan, Kamakura Period, ca. 1300. 53.1

The Poet Taira-No-Kanemori. Section of a handscroll, black and white and slight color on paper. Japan, Kamakura Period, 1185-1333. 51.397

Fukutomi Zoshi. Handscroll, ink and color on paper. Japan, 14th-15th century. 53.358

Yuzu Nembutsu Engi: Efficacy of Repeated Invocations to the Amida Buddha (detail). Handscroll, ink and color and gold on paper. Japan, Kamakura Period, 14th century. 56.87

White-Robed Kwannon from Kozan-ji. Hanging scroll, ink on paper. Japan, late Kamakura Period, ca. 1200. 51.540

278

Choyo: Priest Sewing under the Morning Sun. Hanging scroll, ink on paper. Kao, Japanese, ca. 1350 or slightly earlier, Kamakura Period. 62.163

Haboku Landscape. Hanging scroll, ink on paper. Sesshu, Japanese, 1420-1506, Muromachi Period. 55.43

Winter and Spring Landscape. Six-fold screen, ink and slight color on paper. Shubun, Abbot of Shokoku-ji, Kyoto, Japanese, ca. 1390-1464, Muromachi Period. 58.476*

Birds and Flowers in a Winter and Spring Landscape. One of a pair of six-fold screens, ink and color on paper. Attributed to Sesshu, Japanese, 1420-1506, Muromachi Period. 61.204

Eight Scenes of Hsiao-Hsiang. Dated ca. 1509. Hanging scroll, ink on paper. So-ami, Japanese, Muromachi Period. 63.262*

Horses and Grooms. One of a pair of six-fold screens, color and ink on paper. Japan, Muromachi Period. 1368-1573. 34.374

Dragon and Tiger. Pair of six-fold screens, ink on paper. Sesson, Japanese, born 1504-active until 1589, Muromachi-Ashikaga Periods. 59.136, 59.137*

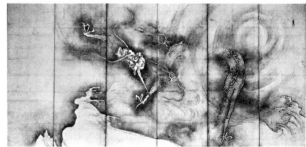

Namban Byobu: Foreign Barbarian Scenes. One of a pair of six-fold screens, color on paper. Japan, datable to 1610-1614. 60.193

Table. Wood, lacquer, gold, and silver. Japan, Muromachi Period, 15th century. 58.429

Cosmetic Box. Lacquer. Japan, Momoyama Period, 1573-1615. 66.25

Bowl with Cross. Glazed stoneware,
Hagi ware. Japan, Momoyama Period,
ca. 1600. 62.211

Dish with Design of Flying Geese.
Stoneware, Shino ware. Japan,
Momoyama Period, 1573-1615. 59.35

Ewer. Pottery, Oribe ware. Japan,
Momoyama Period, 1573-1615. 58.336

Dish. Stoneware, Shino ware. Japan, Momoyama Period, 1573-1615. 66.24

Scene from the Ise Monogatari: The Beach at Sumiyoshi. Album painting, color and gold on paper. Early 17th century. Nonomura Sotatsu, Japanese, Edo Period. 51.398

Sano-no-Watari: Crossing at Sano. Screen, ink on gold-ground paper. Early 17th century. Sotatsu, Japanese, Edo Period. 49.554

Chrysanthemums by a Stream. One of a pair of six-fold screens, color and gold leaf on paper. Ogata Korin, Japanese, 1658-1716, Tokugawa Period. 58.207

Utsunoyama: The Pass Through the Mountains. Six-fold screen, color on gold-ground paper. Fukaye Roshu, Japanese, 1699-1755, Edo Period. 54.127*

Calligraphy by Koetsu Written over Designs by Sotatsu.
Ink, gold, silver, and color on paper. Japan, early
17th century, Edo Period. 66.118

Irises. One of a pair of six-fold screens, ink and color on
gold ground over paper. Watanabe Shiko, Japanese,
1683-1755, Edo Period. 54.604

Thirty-six Poets. Two-fold screen, color on paper.
1st half 18th century. Attributed to Tatebayashi Kagei,
Japanese, Edo Period. 60.183

Paulownias and Chrysanthemums. Two-fold screen, color
and gold on paper. Hoitsu, Japanese, 1761-1828, Edo Period.
64.386

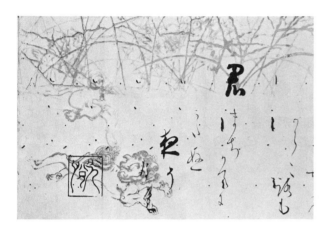

Bamboo in Fine Weather After Rain. Two-fold screen, ink on paper. Ike-no-Taiga, Japanese, 1723-1776, late Edo Period. 58.337

Beauties in a Garden. Six-fold screen, color and gold on paper. Japan, early Edo Period, style of Matabei, mid-17th century. 64.352

Forbidden to the Vulgar. Hanging scroll, ink on paper. Gyokudo, Japanese, 1745-1820, Edo Period. 64.367

The Actor Sanjo Kantaro. Color on paper. Ca. 1714. Kaigetsudo Ando, Japanese, Edo Period. 61.41

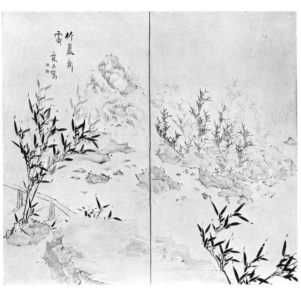

Tzuzuri Bako: Writing Box. Lacquer. Japan, Edo Period, ca. 1800. 63.260

Covered Bowl with Chrysanthemums and Chidori. Porcelain, Kakiemon ware, decorated in colored enamels. Japan, Edo Period, early 18th century. 61.42

Standing Figure of a Beauty. Porcelain, Kakiemon ware. Japan, Edo Period, late 17th century. 64.366*

Plate with Bird and Flower. Porcelain, Kutani ware. Japan, Edo Period, 17th century. 60.174

Bowl (one of a pair). Porcelain, Kakiemon ware. Japan, Edo Period, late 17th century. 64.364

Notes

Notes

Notes

Pre-Columbian Art

290

Jade Figurine. Mexico, Gulf Coast,
Olmec, before A.D. 300. 41.390*

Stone Axe. Mexico, Gulf Coast, Olmec,
before 300. 54.856

Seated Figure. Stone. Mexico, Gulf
Coast, Olmec, before 300. 51.179

Stone Head. Mexico, Olmec style,
1st-5th century. 53.369

Jade Head. Mexico, Western Mexico(?)
Olmec style, 1st-5th century. 61.31

291

Recumbent Anthropomorphic Figure. Stone. Mexico, Gulf Coast, 3rd-5th century(?). 48.355

Terra-cotta Head. Mexico, Gulf Coast, Totonac or Tajin, 5th-9th century. 40.11*

Painted Terra-cotta Head. Mexico, Gulf Coast, Totonac or Tajin, 5th-9th century. 47.26

Dog. Earthenware. Mexico, Colima, 6th-7th century(?). 64.37

Seated Figure. Terra cotta. Mexico, Oaxaca, Monte Alban II (Zapotec), before Christ(?). 54.857*

Monkey. Stone. Mexico, Tacubaya, Aztec, 15th century. 59.125

Gold Shell with Bells. Mexico, Oaxaca, Mixtec, after 1000. 52.86

Xochipilli, God of Flowers, Dance, and Games. Stone. Mexico, Aztec, 15th century. 49.555

Stone Head. Honduras, Copan, Maya, 7th-8th century. 53.154

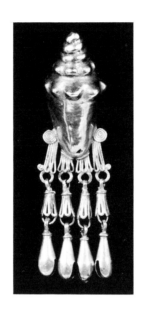

293

Seated Figure. Incised shell. Guatemala, Maya, 3rd-5th century. 65.550*

Woman in Ceremonial Robes. Limestone relief. Mexico or Guatemala, Usumacinta Region, Maya, ca. 795. 62.32*

Incense Burner. Terra cotta. Mexico, Palenque Region, 7th-8th century. 65.248*

Vase. Earthenware with painted decoration. Guatemala, Kixpee, Maya, 8th-10th century. 54.391

Figure of a Warrior. Terra cotta. Mexico, Yucatan, Island of Guaymil, Maya, 9th-10th century. 63.93

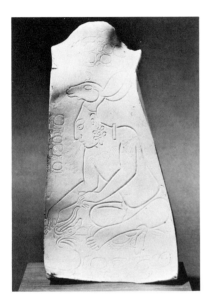

294

Left: *Jade Head.* Honduras, Copan, Maya, 7th-8th century. 47.176
Center: *Jade Pendant.* Mexico or Central America, Maya, 6th-8th century. 52.119
Right: *Plaque.* Crystalline green stone. Mexico or Central America, Maya, 7th-9th century. 50.153

Eccentric Flint in Human Shape.
Stone. Guatemala, Quirigua, Maya,
6th-8th century. 50.161*

Jaguar Macehead. Stone. Costa Rica,
Nicoya, Chorotegan, 8th-9th century.
49.469

Gold Plaque. Panama, Coclé,
14th-15th century. 52.459*

Anthropomorphic Seated Figure.
Gold. Colombia, Quimbaya, 14th-15th
century. 39.509*

Double Puma Staff Head. Gold.
Colombia, Quimbaya, 14th-15th
century. 44.319

Bird (Head of a Staff?). Gold. Colombia,
Quimbaya, 14th-15th century. 54.594

Gold Pin. Colombia, Quimbaya,
14th-15th century. 47.30

Gold Spoon. Peru, North Coast,
Chavin, 1st millennium B.C. 58.177*

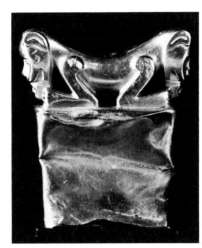

296

Gold Plaque. Peru, North Coast, Chavin, 1st millennium B.C. 46.117

Finial in the Form of a Monkey. Gold. Peru, North Coast, Mochica, 1st-5th century. 49.197

Bowl with Incised Decoration. Stone. Peru, North Coast, Chavin, 1st millennium B.C. 55.167

Border of a Mantle (detail). Painted cotton. Peru, South Coast, Early Period. 40.530*

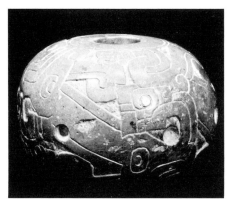

297

Poncho. Needle réseau, wool. Peru, South Coast, Paracas, Early Period. 40.514

Part of a Mantle (detail). Embroidery, wool. Peru, South Coast, Paracas, Early Period. 40.528

Mosaic Relief. Peru, North (?) Coast, Tiahuanaco, 9th-10th century. 44.291

Poncho. Embroidery, wool. Peru, South Coast, Paracas, Early Period. 46.227

Jar. Earthenware with painted decoration. Peru, South Coast, Tiahuanaco, 10th-12th century. 55.173

Poncho. Tapestry weave, wool and cotton. Peru, South Coast, Tiahuanaco Culture, Middle Period. 56.84

Textile. Tapestry weave, wool and cotton. Peru, South Coast, Tiahuanaco Culture, Middle Period. 57.495

Square Hat. Pile knot technique, wool. Peru, South Coast, Middle Period. 45.378

299

Front of a Litter. Peru, North Coast, Chimu, 12th-13th century. 52.233*

Poncho. Tapestry weave, wool and cotton. Peru, South Coast, Inca Culture, 1400-1532. 57.136

Half Poncho. Tapestry weave, wool and cotton. Peru, Inca Period, 16th century. 51.393

Notes

Art of Primitive Peoples

Mule's Head fom a Headpiece. **Wood** and metal. Africa, Republic of **Mali,** Bambara Tribe. 35.307

Woman and Child (Maternity Figure). Wood. Africa, Ivory Coast, Korhogo District, Senufo Tribe. 61.198

Dance Mask (Satimbe?). Wood. Africa, Republic of Mali, Sanga District, Dogon Tribe. 60.169

Miniature Mask. Cast gold. Africa, Ivory Coast, Baule Tribe. 54.602

Snake. Painted wood. Africa, Guinea, Baga Tribe, Landouman Sub-tribe. 60.

Warrior-Attendant Plaque. Bronze. Africa, Nigeria, Benin, 17th century. 53.425

303

Altar Portrait of a Deceased Oba.
Bronze. Africa, Nigeria, Benin, 17th
century. 38.6

Dance Mask. Painted wood. Africa,
Republic of the Congo, Kasai Province,
Bushongo Tribe (Bakuba). 35.304*

Pair of Lions. Wood. Africa, Dahomey. 65.323-65.324

War Shield. Painted wood. Melanesia, Dutch New Guinea, Asmat. 63.554

Lintel. Wood. Polynesia, New Zealand, Maori. 62.350

Kamanggabi Figure. Painted wood with cowrie-shell. Melanesia, New Guinea, Central Sepik River District, Arambak. 63.553

Canoe Prow. Wood. Southeast New Guinea, Massim Area, Trobriand Islands, 19th century. 66.130

Ceremonial Adze. Wood, stone, fiber. Central Polynesia, Hervey Islands. 40.1078

Staff (U'u) (detail). Stained ironwood. Polynesia, Marquesas Islands. 63.255

Yoke. Wood. Polynesia, Easter Island. 61.406

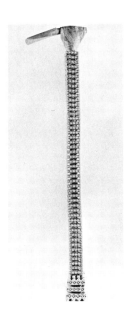

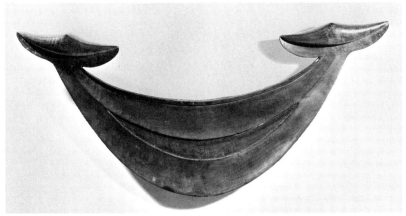

Notes